planning and assessing the curriculum in English Language Arts

Stephen Tchudi

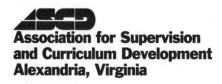

Association for Supervision
and Curriculum Development
Alexandria, Virginia

Printed in the United States of America.
Printed by: Book Press, Inc.
Typeset by: Valerie Sprague
Cover design by: Keith Demmons

Ronald S. Brandt, *Executive Editor*
Nancy Modrak, *Managing Editor, Books*
Ginger R. Miller, *Associate Editor*
Gary Bloom, *Manager, Design and Production Services*

Price: $13.95
ASCD Stock Number: 611-91150
ISBN:0-87120-185-2

Library of Congress Cataloging-in-Publication Data

Tchudi, Stephen, 1942–
  Planning and assessing the curriculum in English language arts / Stephen Tchudi.
    p.   cm.
  Includes bibliographical references.
  ISBN 0-87120-185-2
  1. Language arts—United States—Curricula.   2. Language arts—United States—
Curricula—Case studies.   3. English language—Study and teaching—United States—
Curricula.   I. Title.
LB1576.T3585   1991
375.428—dc20   91-26547
                                                                              CIP

Planning and Assessing the Curriculum in English Language Arts

Foreword

There is no doubt that the world is getting smaller as technology increases the ways people communicate. The English language arts curriculum is a key tool for helping students understand and be understood in this multicultural, information-rich world.

This year, ASCD passed a resolution stating that "information literacy, the ability to locate, process, and use information effectively, equips individuals to take advantage of the opportunities inherent in the global information society." The English language arts curriculum is the ideal place to teach the varied skills of information literacy. The importance of this curriculum is attested to by the fact that schools require students to take courses in English language arts every year from kindergarten through senior high school.

Many educators have attempted to describe the ideal English language arts curriculum. No one has succeeded. In this book, Stephen Tchudi resists the natural urge to single-handedly prescribe a solution for the challenges facing English language arts educators. Instead, he provides readers with processes for designing, implementing, and evaluating curriculums suited to the needs of individual schools and students. He suggests that curriculum developers think of the curriculum as a three-ring binder, allowing lessons, like binder pages, to be frequently added, deleted, and modified. His beliefs are supported by examples from around the United States and research from schools and professional associations.

In this age of rapid information exchange, the English language arts curriculum must provide students with an appreciation of language arts and the ability to use these skills to learn and communicate. During my years as a district supervisor of English language arts I realized above all that there is no one right way to teach this curriculum. English language arts instruction must take into account the individual child, his grade level, ability, and learning style. And in the end, teaching for the transfer of skills is our most crucial challenge.

Corrine Hill
ASCD President
1991-1992

Introduction

When ASCD asked me to write a book on English language arts curriculums, my first impulse was to follow my own (and many other educators') dream and to produce a comprehensive, idealized, presumably visionary English program that could be adopted by K-12 schools nationwide and serve them effectively from now to eternity. But my experience in various curriculum development groups and my understanding of evolving English programs led me in a different direction.

This book concerns *processes* for program development, and it strongly resists the notion that there is a single curriculum—local, state, or national—that all other schools can or should follow. Rather, I have chosen to focus on philosophical and practical issues in program development, proposing that if curriculum leaders have a full understanding of current language learning theory and if they follow sound procedures in developing programs, the final curriculum *products* will themselves be outstanding.

Part One of this book provides the theoretical underpinnings for this approach to curriculum. I begin with a historical overview of the evolution of English language arts programs to help curriculum developers understand past traditions and assumptions. I then describe the origins of a "new English" that has been emerging over the past three decades and outline what seem to be its most promising characteristics.

Part Two presents current curriculums and patterns of development. Here I solicited help from teachers and curriculum leaders in the field. One chapter reports a survey of national Centers of Excellence in English where curriculum makers describe the processes that led to their successful programs. A second chapter presents first-person narratives by curriculum leaders from Fairbanks, Alaska; Midland, Michigan; Hampton, Virginia; and Houston, Texas. Here readers will find descriptions of a range of particular (and common) curriculum problems: responding to community criticism, selecting texts consistent with new directions, organizing large curriculum teams, overcoming faculty inertia, and keeping up enthusiasm when things look glum.

Part Three, A Curriculum Developer's Handbook, gets down to the nuts-and-bolts of curriculum engineering. Here I offer a variety of tasks and projects that individual curriculum developers and curriculum teams can undertake. My suggestions will, I hope, prompt most curriculum writers to develop other, individually appropriate tasks for themselves.

I want to give particular thanks to my four colleagues who wrote the curriculum narratives for Chapter 4: Lillian Hassler, Carol Kuykendall, Jan Loveless, and Betty Swiggett. Their contributions help put the teeth in this book and save it from being an academic, ivory tower exercise.

Much of my thinking about curriculum-as-process was shaped when I served as chair of the Committee on the Michigan Secondary School Curriculum, and I appreciate the input and debate provided by the members of that group.

Finally, I want to thank Ron Brandt for the invitation to write and ASCD for its interest in English language arts curriculums.

—Stephen Tchudi
University of Nevada, Reno

PART ONE

The English Language Arts Curriculum in the 1990s

1 | Historical Roots

Although this book is principally concerned with present-day English language arts curriculums and with ways of developing more successful programs in the future, it begins with an historical overview because instruction in the mother tongue has been a part of American schools since colonial times. Reading and writing constituted two-thirds of the curriculum in the schools established by the Massachusetts Bay Colony in 1848. For the colonists, literacy was akin to godliness, providing access to the sacred word of the Bible. Reading and writing, coupled with arithmetic, also offered opportunities for success in the colonial world of commerce, permitting people to keep ledgers, to write invoices, and to prepare agreements, in short, to use numbers and letters in the service of financial gain. In many respects, those twin foci have remained a part of today's language arts programs, which are broadly conceived as providing practical life skills along with access to culture and traditional values.

Language instruction in the colonial schools was a "curriculum" packaged between the covers of a slim little volume, *The New England Primer*. In about one hundred pages, the *Primer* presented reading and writing to generations of children (and indirectly, to adults) using an alphabetic approach that is the distant ancestor of today's phonics lessons (Ford 1962). Students were first taught the shapes and sounds of the alphabet through mnemonic verses: "In Adam's fall, we sinn'd all." "Xerxes the king did die, and so must you and I." Next, children were shown how to build syllables from vowels and consonants: "ba," "be," "bi," "bo," "bu." Words were created from the stock of syllables, short words for the younger children, longer and more difficult ones for the older students. The method was simple and direct, if mechanistic.

The New England Primer contained its own reading matter as well, most of it religious and moralistic. Texts included religious catechism, stories of Biblical heroes and heroines, letters from church leaders addressed to children, and advice about persevering in one's studies. In a sense, the *Primer* was more of a speller than either a reading or writing book because it assumed that knowing how to spell allowed one to both decode and encode language.

Today's English language arts curriculum builder might cast an envious glance at the *Primer* because of its remarkable brevity and compactness. We recognize that part of the charm of the book grew from its simplistic pedagogy. However, in the twentieth century, *Primer*-style pedagogy, dedicated instruction in sound-letter correspondence, has been criticized as a system that may actually inhibit the development of reading skills. Today, writing is more complicated than keeping notes and records; reading is much more complex than simply pronouncing the words one can spell. Successful language use today includes computers and telephones as well as books, paper, and pencils. It involves oral language as well as print and includes complex skills relating learning, thinking, and knowing. Although one occasionally hears a call for a return to *Primer* pedagogy, twentieth century language teaching has evolved far beyond the simple drills and recitations of colonial New England.

As the English language arts curriculum has expanded, so has our conception of "good" or "successful" language use. We have come to understand that learning language is extraordinarily complex. Some elements of the curriculum have been added because of public pressure; others have come about through the influence of college entrance examinations; still others have entered as a result of new pedagogical conceptions of language and learning. English has sometimes created its own pedagogy, and sometimes it has borrowed from fields as different as classical languages and mathematics. Seldom has anything been deleted, so that today's typical English language arts program often represents conflicting aims and methodologies. That "typical" curriculum is a mythical beast, of course, but one can see its footprints in the hallways of virtually any elementary or secondary school in America.

English teachers have taken arms against their curricular dragon from time to time, and they have scored some direct hits. For example, we no longer teach literature through etymological analysis of word origins. Teachers have also lopped off Hydra-like appendages from time to time, often to see them regenerate, as in the case of teaching formal grammar.

To understand this curricular dragon and to contemplate strategies for taming it, we need to take a look at how the English curriculum has developed in the years since *The New England Primer*.

The Tradition in Language Instruction

When I took an English methods class in 1963, the English curriculum was described as a tripod: three legs representing *literature*, *language*, and *composition*. Exploring that metaphor, the instructor reminded us that the legs of a tripod needed to be of the same length or else it would fall over. Thus, the three parts of English deserved equal emphasis. My own observations as a new high school teacher persuaded me that the tripod was already out of balance. The literature leg was long and stout. (Every English teacher liked to teach and talk about stories, poems, plays, and novels.) The composition leg was a mere stub. (Nobody wanted to grade papers!) Language was a leafless twig represented by the sentence diagram. (Most teachers "did" grammar, including some diagramming, but few people—especially the students—were persuaded that it was doing very much good.)

What I had encountered was what English curriculum specialists call "the traditional approach." There was little integration of the three components of the tripod so that "lit" "lang," and "comp" were taught in isolation from one another. The three components did, however, share a broad common approach to pedagogy: They were "knowledge" or "content" centered. That is, the fundamental teaching principle behind "the tradition" held that the teacher must present knowledge of the elements of language, writing, and literature and then ask students to apply that knowledge. At the secondary school level, the study of literature centered on a series of introductions to literature, including the basics of poetry, prose, fiction, and nonfiction; the cultural heritage of British, American, and world literature; and knowledge of literary facts and terminology such as plot, character, and poetic forms. Writing—when taught—concentrated on the forms of exposition in carefully designed paragraphs. The aim of language instruction was grammatical and mechanical.

The tripod was, indeed, out of balance, because each of its legs had been developed independently, at different periods of history. The language leg, for example, was a late eighteenth and early nineteenth century addition to the curriculum, coming into the schools some 125 years after *The New England Primer*. Through best-selling books like Lindlay Murray's (1795) *English Grammar*, children memorized parts of speech, recited laws of sentence construction, and "parsed"—presenting detailed descriptions of the grammar.

In the late nineteenth century, parsing was replaced by sentence diagramming, but the pedagogical assumption, largely unchallenged until our own time, was that knowledge of the rules of grammar led to improved performance in language. Murray summed it up by saying that grammar "*is* the art of speaking and writing with propriety." In his mind (and in the minds of generations of teachers), there was no distinction between knowing the "laws" of language and being able to use language correctly.

The composition leg of the tripod was created about fifty years later. Students were taught "laws" of rhetoric and practiced them on set theme topics such as "The Good Man," "The Important Virtues," or "My Trip to _____." These student compositions were used by the teacher to discover errors, which the student would slavishly correct. The infamous "red pencil" came into common use during this period as a tool for highlighting students' gramatical and rhetorical failings.

The literature leg of the curriculum, hefty as it was, turned out to be a laminate of two separate traditions: reading and literature. *Reading* had been a part of the language arts program from the very beginning. The religious tone of school reading material diminished over time as *The New England Primer* was gradually replaced by texts with a more secular content, most notably, the McGuffey readers (Lindbergh 1976, Windhover 1978). *Literature* became established toward the end of the nineteenth century.

5

Interest in literature developed rapidly (Applebee 1974) with English and American literature gaining a foothold in the secondary schools as a core component of instruction. The development of college entrance examinations toward the end of the nineteenth century further supported the development of literature instruction as the colleges mandated or set particular books for candidacy examinations. In this way, the English curriculum picked up such standbys as Shakespeare's *As You Like It* and *The Merchant of Venice*, Dickens' *A Tale of Two Cities* and *David Copperfield*, and George Eliot's *Silas Marner*.

In 1893, the National Education Association issued a landmark *Report of the Committee of Ten* (NEA 1893) on the teaching of various school subjects. English was described as a subject second to none in importance in the elementary and secondary schools. It was approved as a K-12 required component of instruction, occupying a larger share of the curriculum than mathematics, science, or history. The curriculum model implicit in the *Committee of Ten* report was that of the tripod. Thus, when I first taught school in 1963, I inherited a curriculum that had been formed in the nineteenth century and had been in place for more than seventy years (Tchudi 1978, Mason 1978).

Progressivism and the Teaching of English

There have been attempts to overturn the traditional curriculum, to tip over the tripod in favor of other models. Patricia Cavanaugh (1990) has shown that, since 1870, progressive educators have argued that the traditional approach to language arts has been inappropriately centered on the study of rules, laws, and academic content. For three-quarters of a century, men and women like Francis Parker, John Dewey, Hughes Mearns, Rudolf Steiner, and Laura Zirbes argued that English instruction ignored the needs, interests, and developing skills of the child, and that it ignored the organic unity of language, which flows naturally from reading to writing to listing to speaking.

The most influential curriculum document to emerge from this movement, one which, for a time, seriously threatened the traditional curriculum, was NCTE's *An Experience Curriculum in English* (Hatfield 1935). This program emphasized language activities rather than knowledge of language; its pedagogical password was "learning by doing." The *Experience Curriculum* linked reading, writing, and speaking through language experiences that were designed to accomplish social as well as academic tasks. A companion volume, *A Correlated Curriculum* (NCTE 1935), showed how an organic view of language could create links to other school disciplines, a concept similar to that of today's language-across-the-curriculum movement.

In the end, neither of these volumes nor the progressive movement itself had success in displacing the traditional curriculum. The disruption of World War II focused the energies of teachers on other matters (England 1978) and like many of the recommendations of the progressive educators in all fields, it was seen by many critics as being "soft" both on content and discipline.

The Debate over Content

In the 1950s, critics like Rudolf Flesch and Hyman Rickover attacked the schools in general and the language arts in particular for their progressive methodologies. In his classic book, *Why Johnny Can't Read—And What You Can Do About It*, Flesch (1955) lamented what he perceived to be a decline in phonics instruction (the descendent of *New England Primer* alphabetic teaching) in favor of "look-say" or whole-word teaching (a very distant ancestor of today's whole-language methods). He properly critiqued the banality of texts like the "Dick and Jane" books with their legendary dog, Spot, but he confused the readers with their methodology and failed to understand the pedagogy behind look-say.

Critics like Flesch gained a good deal of support in the press when Sputnik was launched by the Soviet Union in 1957. Newspapers were filled with discussion of an allegedly scandalous state of affairs in U.S. schools. The language arts, like other fields, experienced a period of curricular reassessment. In the early 1960s, English educators, like mathematics and science educators, joined in a quest for new curriculums and teaching methods.

Federally sponsored Project English centers were created to design new programs. The first order of business was to examine the history of the English curriculum, which led to the discovery that, by and large, the traditional approach had failed. For example, dozens of studies attempting to link grammar instruction to improved writing failed to find significant improvement. Instruction in paragraph structures, expository themes, and research papers had not produced good writers. In addition, the teaching of reading was overemphasizing comprehension and subskills and was not yielding fluent, active readers. Despite its prominence in the curriculum, literature instruction wasn't doing very well either. Approaches to literature were found to be overly academic, focusing on mastery of names, dates, and terminology rather than on the reader's engagement with a text.

The Project English movement encouraged English language arts teachers to critically reexamine their aims and methods. Thus, in the mid-1960s, English instruction and research began a quest to find its disciplinary center (North 1987).

A New Progressivism

In the 1960s, the language arts were awash in new formulations of the discipline: a "new" grammar, a "new" rhetoric, new ways of perceiving literary structure. The tradition and the tripod fell into disfavor, and two important curriculum ideas gained prominence. One of these—the "growth through English" movement—remains influential and is discussed in the next chapter. This pedagogy has some clear links to progressivism, but draws on a considerably more sophisticated view of language and learning.

7

The second movement, one exclusive to the secondary schools, deserves discussion not only because of its content, but also because it ultimately failed.

In 1968, the professional journals first carried references to a new model: "elective" curriculums for high schools. The idea was to do away with traditional courses labeled English I, II, III, and IV, each with its garbled mix of literature, language, and composition, and to create a variety of shorter courses—some as short as three-week mini-courses—in which students could focus on particular literatures, language study, or creative or expository writing. Electives were seen as student-centered because they provided students with a range of choices of what to study. Further, electives could be "phased" by difficulty, doing away with the need for tracked classes by letting students opt into the program at the level *they* felt was appropriate.

Electives took the country by storm. The movement spread so rapidly that in 1972 the NCTE published a critical appraisal of such programs, written by George Hillocks, a professor at the University of Chicago. Hillocks found that, nationwide, elective programs offered a dizzying array of course titles. He observed that elective courses opened up the content of English, moving beyond traditional selections in British and American literature to include such literatures as science fiction, sports, media, and even the supernatural. However, he also observed that many of the elective titles sounded like college courses. He questioned whether courses such as Shakespeare, drama, poetry, and a survey of British literature genuinely reflected student interests, and he noted that traditional course titles outnumbered most of the snazzier student-centered topics. In short, there was some evidence that electives could give the appearance of curriculum reform without resulting in substantive changes in pedagogy.

Nevertheless, Hillocks (1972) concluded that elective curriculums had a powerful effect in energizing teachers, who were

> . . . no longer content to be controlled by an outmoded curriculum. They (with the advice of their students) want to control the curriculum. Given the time to study, plan, and evaluate their work, English teachers, with their newly awakened sense of professional dignity and responsibility, may manage to revolutionize the teaching of English for all students .

The revolution Hillocks anticipated never materialized. A back-to-basics movement and a thrust toward career education in the mid-1970s, coupled with increased interest in state and national testing, terminated elective programs in the secondary schools as rapidly as they began. Worry about declining college entrance test scores led taxpayers to perceive electives as having some of the same faults as the earlier progressive movement. Electives were believed to be soft on content and too easy on students. Courses such as "sports literature" and "supernatural literature" were held up as examples of how standards in English had slipped. By the end of the 1970s, electives were disappearing rapidly; by the mid-1980s there were just vestiges of the elective system such as an occasional course in drama or reading for pleasure.

Back to Cultural Basics

In 1984, the national report *A Nation at Risk* galvanized parents and educators with its warning of a "rising tide of mediocrity" in education. The longer school days and years of Japanese schools were described favorably in contrast to the American system. Model school curriculums proposed by then-Secretary of Education William Bennett (1987) were strong on traditional core subjects. E. D. Hirsch (1987) of the University of Virginia wrote his best-selling book, *Cultural Literacy*, which lamented what he saw as decaying levels of common or core knowledge.

I believe that critics like Bennett and Hirsch err in arguing for a return to the imagined glories of traditional schooling. In English language arts classes, at least, there is surprising uniformity and consistent exposure to a more or less common curriculum, the traditional program that has never been mandated or developed by national committees. It is a tradition that is ensconced in the commercial textbooks that arguably dictate the broad outlines of curriculum in most schools. It is also a program that has demonstrably failed to meet its own aims, much less the needs of students.

Those concerned about the literacy curriculum should not be longing for "the good old days" of alleged higher literacy and imagined allegiance to a common culture. Nor should they assume that a national curriculum, perhaps backed by a battery of tests, can change the pattern of instruction. Rather, they should be asking why the unofficial core curriculum of the English language arts has not proven particularly successful throughout its long history. We have to ask why the traditional dragon, despite its wounds, still prowls the halls of many elementary and secondary schools.

References

A Nation at Risk. (1984). Cambridge, Mass.: USA Research.

Applebee, A. (1974). *Tradition and Reform in the Teaching of English: A History.* Urbana, Ill.: National Council of Teachers of English.

Bennett, W. (1987). *James Madison High School.* Washington, D.C.: U.S. Department of Education.

Cavanaugh, M.P. (1990). "The Holistic Teaching Methods of Francis Parker, John Dewey, Rudolf Steiner, Hughes Mearns, and Laura Zirbes: Literacy via the Whole Child." Unpublished doctoral dissertation. East Lansing: Michigan State University.

England, D. (1978). "With Grammar on My Left." *The English Journal* 68, 4: 67-73.

Flesch, R.F. (1955). *Why Johnny Can't Read—And What You Can Do About It.* New York: Harper.

Ford, P.L., ed. (1962). *The New England Primer: A History of Its Origin and Development.* New York: Teachers College, Columbia University.

Hatfield, W.W., chair. (1935). *An Experience Curriculum in English.* New York: National Council of Teachers of English and D. Appleton.

Hillocks, G. (1972). *Alternatives in English: A Critical Appraisal of Elective Programs.* Urbana, Ill.: National Council of Teachers of English.

Hirsch, E.D. (1987). *Cultural Literacy.* Boston, Mass.: Houghton Mifflin.

Lindbergh, S., ed. (1976). *Selections from the McGuffey Eclectic Readers.* New York: Van Nostrand.

Mason, J.H. (1978). "The Educational Milieu, 1874–1911: College Entrance Requirements and the Shaping of Secondary Education." *The English Journal* 68, 4: 40–45.

NEA. (1893). *Report of the Committee of Ten.* Washington, D.C.: National Education Association.

NCTE. (1935). *A Correlated Curriculum.* New York: Appleton, Century, Crofts.

North, S. (1987). *The Making of Knowledge in Composition.* Exeter, N.H.: Boynton/Cook.

Tchudi, S. (April 1978). "Composition and Rhetoric in American Secondary Schools, 1840–1900." *The English Journal* 68, 4: 34-39.

Windhover, R. (1978). "Literature in the Nineteenth Century." *The English Journal* 68, 4: 28-33.

2 | An Emerging New English

Teachers and administrators familiar with new directions in the teaching of the English language arts may consider the preceding chapter pessimistic in its view of the stodginess of English curriculums. Despite the obstacles presented by back-to-basics, the dominance of standardized testing, and the conservative core curriculum movement, there has been enormous growth and development in both the theory and practice of teaching English during the past three decades. In many schools, the traditional dragon has been slain (or at least closeted) and replaced by a "new English" (O'Neill 1989).

The impetus for this new English was a seminar of American and British English teachers held at Dartmouth College in 1966. John Dixon (1968, 1976) of the United Kingdom summarized the nature of the new pedagogy in *Growth Through English*, a title suggestive of the book's pedagogical program. Dixon explained, "From the baby gooing in the cradle to the senior citizen reading the newspaper, people crave language and draw on it constantly to conduct the business of life." Schools must, therefore, provide an arena that fosters language growth. Dixon used a phrase that caught the imagination of teachers when he rejected the concept of "dummy run" or practice exercises. To learn language, he argued, students need to employ it in pursuit of what they see as genuine ends and purposes.

The Dartmouth seminar provided the theoretical base for a curriculum in which students would write frequently for a variety of self-selected and assigned purposes, read for personal growth and enlightenment in a selection of texts written for young people and adults, and strengthen oral language through discussion, drama, and debate.

This model did not spring fully formed from the minds of the Dartmouth seminar participants. The personal growth philosophy had been practiced in some British infant schools since the 1930s, and it had strong connections with

11

Deweyan progressivism in U.S. education. This new model extended both these traditions by incorporating new research on the relationships between learning and thinking, in particular the works of Lev Vygotsky (1962), Susanne Langer (1954), James Britton (1974), and James Moffett (1968).

The Personal Growth Model

The growth-through-English approach operates under several aliases. It is variously called "student centered," "naturalistic," "developmental," "organic," "integrated," "language experience," and "whole language." Each of these names hints at one of the central features of the personal growth model, which:

- looks to the *students'* language as the starting point for instruction;
- allows for *natural* progression of language skill development instead of prescribed sequences;
- builds skills *developmentally*, meshing instruction with students' cognitive and linguistic growth;
- *organically* connects language and literature;
- *integrates* the various components of language arts—reading, writing, listening, and speaking;
- uses youngsters' own *experiences* with life as the entry point for reading and writing; and
- treats language as a *whole*, rather than dividing instruction into discrete skill components.

By 1979, the NCTE's Commission on Curriculum, chaired by Barrett Mandell of Rutgers University, identified the personal growth model as one of three major curriculum approaches in U.S. schools, along with the traditional skills and cultural heritage approaches.

In 1984, at an international conference on English teaching held at Michigan State University, representatives from Australia, Canada, England, New Zealand, and the United States discovered considerable homogeneity of philosophy in the personal growth approach. Conference participants seemed confident that English had found its pedagogical center. There were concerns, however, that social, economic, and political constraints in England, Canada, the United States, and Australia were operating to the detriment of holistic language programs (Tchudi 1985).

In 1987, an English Coalition Conference held under the auspices of the NCTE and the Modern Language Association, reaffirmed the preeminence of the personal growth model (Lloyd-Jones and Lunsford 1989). The participants stressed the need for classes that would draw language skills and processes together and for teachers who would encourage children to explore, think, read, and write about a rich variety of experiences. (A summary statement from the English Coalition Conference is reprinted in Appendix A to provide readers with a concise overview of the principles of the new English.)

New Directions in the Classroom

New English is by no means the exclusive product of seminars and conferences, the stereotyped "agreement among academics" with no reference to classroom practice. Teaching and learning in many language arts classrooms today reflects the growth-through-English philosophy through very powerful grassroots developments. Indeed, as English language arts teachers have discovered new possibilities in their subject, their enthusiasm has led at times to near evangelical movements.

Although current theory calls for integration of English, much curriculum development is coming about through specialized projects that focus on one aspect or another of the English program. Five major movements have emerged in the past two decades, each linked to the umbrella theory of growth through English:

1. Writing as Process

Unquestionably, the most successful recent development in English language arts teaching has been in the teaching of composition. Once the short leg of the English tripod, writing instruction now stands on its own.

The catalyst for this increased teaching of composition has been the concept of "writing as process." As early as 1963, Wallace Douglas of Northwestern University wrote about the complexity of the act of writing, not only the motor skills of penmanship, but the intellectual acts of finding ideas, shaping topics, assessing an audience, and revising works. Douglas explained that conventional composition instruction focused exclusively on teaching children the properties of completed pieces, on structures such as paragraphs, topic sentences, logical analysis, and so on. He reasoned that by helping students learn processes—how to *make* compositions—teachers would naturally lead them to discover the traits of written products.

In 1968, Donald Murray of the University of New Hampshire offered a revolutionary book, *A Writer Teaches Writing*, which shows specific strategies for teaching the stages of the composing process. His influence was extended further by the research of Donald Graves (1983), whose *Writing: Teachers and Children at Work* provided teachers with classroom strategies for a process approach and research findings to support their pedagogy.

Word has spread about new approaches to writing through the National Writing Project, under the leadership of James Gray at the University of California, Berkeley. This program has developed inservice sites in every state in the union and in several other countries. In summer workshops, teachers exchange ideas and techniques for teaching writing, discuss the underlying theory and research supporting those ideas, and learn to conduct inservice programs for fellow teachers.

2. Response to Literature: A New Definition of Reading

Growing in part from the work of Louise Rosenblatt (1968) in literature and Kenneth Goodman (1986) in reading, this approach shows that the meanings readers glean from a text depend, in part, on the experiences brought to the reading. Teachers must be concerned not only with the transfer of content from text to child, but also with the processes the child engages in when making sense of the printed page.

To focus on the process of reading requires that teachers learn about individual students, their backgrounds, their interests, their need to know, and their phase of development in life. Teachers using this approach often favor individualized reading of a variety of texts over the reading of common or core texts, a notion first popularized by Daniel Fader (1966, 1968, 1975).

Traditionally, reading specialists and English language arts teachers have operated independently, but new conceptualizations of reading are helping to bridge that gap, with both groups focusing on the student as "meaning maker."

3. The Range and Content of "Reading"

The new directions in literature and reading squarely contradict the "cultural literacy" notion proposed by E.D. Hirsch (1987). Where Hirsch stresses allegiance to a conventional culture dominated by Western thought, teachers of the English language arts are increasingly searching out literature that reflects the concerns of a wide range of races and cultures, including writings by members of both sexes. Such an approach does not call for an abandonment of traditional culture, but it does say that "cultural literacy" involves diverse peoples from all over the globe. Both *Language Arts* and *The English Journal* now run features describing these literatures, and even college and university faculties (often the slowest to change) are engaged in serious debates over opening the canon of standard works to include a greater range of cultures, writing styles, and points of view.

In addition, literature written for children and young adults has increased in quality and availability in the past several decades. Although children's books have long been used in the schools, teachers now have a choice of an extraordinary range of titles, including specialty books such as wordless picture books, which help nonreaders learn to make sense of books by studying the artwork, and big books, which are oversized copies of good children's literature for sharing with a whole class.

The field of adolescent literature—books for students in their early teens—has gained considerable strength and legitimacy in recent years. The NCTE's Adolescent Literature Assembly has over 2,000 members who explore and publicize the use of young adult books as a transition to standard adult reading and as a valuable reading experience in its own right. Both young adult and children's literature also reflect the concern for multiethnic, multicultural reading materials.

On top of that, teachers have discovered the effectiveness of nonfiction trade books in their classrooms: books about science, mathematics, the arts, hobbies, practical skills, astronomy, other lands, and other cultures. These books, along with reading material in newspapers and magazines, have helped free some teachers from textbook dependency and are often used to supplement the adopted text.

4. Whole Language

Until the mid-1980s, the developments in writing and literature were following parallel but separate courses, despite occasional references to a "reading/writing connection." However, the trends in language arts clearly point to an integration based on an obvious link: that writing itself is a process of reading one's own work and reading is an act of composing. Oral language clearly provides another link as a base for reading and writing. One of the earliest forms of integrated English was the "language experience approach" (Lee and Van Allen 1963). Beginning with oral language, which children master even before entering school, this program ingeniously teaches reading by having children dictate stories, which they then learn to read. The scheme unifies children's experiences and their own vocabulary development as they read and write individually with an adult coach.

More recently, a movement toward "whole language" (Goodman 1986) has led to integration of oral language, reading, and writing. It combines such practices as reading and writing workshops, guided individual reading, and writing from personal experience. Whole-language proponents also advocate "kid watching"; they encourage teachers to develop curriculum plans based on the observed interests, concerns, and abilities of their students. Whole language is making its greatest gains in elementary school classrooms, but its philosophical underpinnings are likely to lead to transformations at the secondary school level as well.

5. Language Across the Curriculum

Another powerful movement toward integration of English came about through interest in reading and writing skills throughout the whole curriculum. The seminal research in this area was done in England in the early 1970s (Britton et. al 1974), but the movement quickly caught on in the United States. In its simplest terms, language across the curriculum argues that English is naturally interdisciplinary, that language is generally best learned when it is "about something else," whether the content be history, science, math, or one's personal experiences.

Language across the curriculum invites teachers in other disciplines to use some of the techniques of the new English, such as writing workshops or reading-for-meaning-making. Often, content teachers discover that enhanced learning takes place through reading and writing. Language across the curriculum, then, is not just a matter of getting other teachers to share the teaching of language; it is a fundamentally helpful way to improve learning in the schools.

Whatever Happened to Grammar?

It is easy to see that the traditional model of English instruction has undergone major transformations. Reading and writing are increasingly being merged through such ideas as whole language and language across the curriculum, a union made possible by our increased understanding of language as a way of conducting human affairs.

But what happened to the third leg of the traditional tripod, the language or "grammar" leg? Is it true (as the media seem to think) that English language arts teachers have tossed out grammar, and along with it vocabulary, spelling, linguistic standards, and the pledge of allegiance? How does the new English handle matters of correctness and standards? These are crucial questions, and failure to satisfactorily respond to them can bring English curriculum development to a dead stop.

The teaching of formal schoolroom grammar has certainly decreased in American schools, though there is probably far more grammar being taught than many English education specialists would care to admit. The new approach places correctness within the province of the writing program, specifically, as an editing skill. Rather than ignoring correctness, the personal growth model takes it up at the point where it matters most: after students have composed their ideas and before they are ready to turn in finished, polished products. Skills of correctness are likely to be taught as students encounter particular problems in their writing.

The whole-language context teaches many language skills. Vocabulary grows through extensive reading and experimentation with language rather than through separate instruction. Spelling is mastered through writing and through encountering new words in reading. And most of the discrete language skills that make up language handbooks are organically subsumed in a whole-language, reading/writing approach.

From a broader, theoretical perspective, what was once the rather narrow study of English grammar has been enlarged into a foundation on which new language programs are based. Language is more than good speech or proper writing. It involves composing one's thoughts, learning how to understand others' ideas in speech and writing, developing confidence in one's ability to communicate in various settings, and being able to understand the languages of the mass media. Language, then, is not ignored at all in the new programs. It is at the heart of children's growth through English.

References

Britton, J., and others. (1974). *Keeping Options Open—Writing and the Humanities.* University of London: Institute of Education and the Schools Council.

Dixon, J. (1968, 1976). *Growth Through English.* Urbana, Ill.: National Council of Teachers of English.

Douglas, W. (1963). *An Introduction to Some Lessons in the Basic Processes of Composition.* Evanston, Ill.: Northwestern University Curriculum Study Center in English.

Fader, D., and E. McNeil. (1975). *Hooked on Books: Program and Proof.* New York: Berkeley Medallion.

Goodman, K. (1986). *What's Whole in Whole Language?* Richmond Hill, Ontario: Scholastic.

Graves, D. (1983). *Writing: Teachers and Children at Work.* Exeter, N.H.: Heinemann.

Hirsch, E.D. (1987). *Cultural Literacy.* Boston, Mass.: Houghton Mifflin.

Langer, S. (1954). *Philosophy in a New Key.* Cambridge, Mass.: Harvard.

Lee, D., and R. Van Allen. (1963). *Learning to Read Through Experience.* New York: Appleton, Century, Crofts.

Lloyd-Jones, R., and A. Lunsford, eds. (1989). *The English Coalition Conference: Democracy Through Language.* Urbana, Ill.: National Council of Teachers of English.

Mandell, B.J., ed. (1979). *Three Language Arts Curriculum Models: Pre-Kindergarten Through College.* Urbana, Ill.: National Council of Teachers of English.

Moffett, J. (1968). *Teaching the Universe of Discourse.* Boston, Mass.: Houghton Mifflin.

Murray, D. (1968). *A Writer Teaches Writing.* Boston, Mass.: Houghton Mifflin.

O'Neill, J. (1989). "'Whole Language': New View of Literacy Gains in Influence." *ASCD Update* 31, 1: 6-7.

Rosenblatt, L. (1968). *Literature as Exploration.* New York: Noble and Noble.

Tchudi, S., ed. (1985). *Language, Schooling and Society.* Portsmouth, N.H.: Boyton/Cook.

Vygotsky, L. (1962). *Thought and Language.* Cambridge, Mass.: MIT Press.

PART TWO

Successful Curriculum Development in the English Language Arts

3 | Centers of Excellence in English

A good language arts curriculum.
Some schools have one. Some don't.

Sometimes excellent programs emerge from committees who work carefully for years discussing professional issues and the selection of materials. At other times an outstanding curriculum seems to be the exclusive product of an inspired and energetic individual teacher. Although English teachers often talk about the contents of good programs, the professional literature does not offer many insights into the "process of composing" that most elusive of genres: the English language arts curriculum.

A relatively new project of the National Council of Teachers of English is helping to fill this void. In 1984, responding to allegations of a "rising tide of mediocrity," as described in *A Nation at Risk*, NCTE searched for models of excellence in English language arts instruction. Since then, its Centers of Excellence program has identified many schools that have exemplary projects.

The centers program is not a curriculum contest, not a Grammy Awards of the English teaching industry. It identifies, documents, and publicizes programs that represent the best of current English language arts practice. Schools who believe they have something special to offer apply for recognition by describing their program: its rationale, its particular strengths, and the evidence of its success. Submissions are screened by a Committee on Centers of Excellence of NCTE, whose members evaluate the proposals by such criteria as the fullness and accuracy of the program description, consistency with current theory and research in the language arts, length of operation of the program, and innovative or imaginative approaches to problems of teaching and learning language. The Committee then sponsors a site visit by selected NCTE members who verify that the program functions as stated in the school's applications. In the 1987-89 program cycle, nearly 700 schools or districts applied for recognition; 132 were identified as Centers of Excellence.

To gain insights into the process of English curriculum development, I sent a survey (Figure 3.1) to the contact person in each of the Centers of Excellence. Of the 127 centers still in operation at the end of 1989 (five had either completed operation, folded, or been incorporated into other school or district programs), fifty-one replied to my survey. (The participating schools and contact people are acknowledged in Appendix D.) The responding centers have undertaken a wide range of curriculum projects. Thirteen focus on development of a complete English or language arts curriculum either for a K-12 system or for an elementary, junior high/middle school, or senior high school program. The junior high/middle school programs included reading centers, writing centers and labs, integrated studies, humanities, and integrated reading and writing. Among senior high schools, projects included several variations of humanities and interdisciplinary programs, special education, career English, elective programs, grade nine introductory English, writing labs, writing tutors, speech in English, computer-assisted writing, flexible scheduling, and programs for less able students. The remaining senior high school projects centered on one aspect of literacy instruction, for example, composition, reading, or language. At the elementary level, focuses included whole-language and integrated language arts instruction, the use of computers in writing, "real" book programs, interdisciplinary curriculum, and staff development in teaching literature.

Reflecting the great national interest in writing of the 1980s, twenty-two projects focused on some aspect of writing development, for example, creating a new writing curriculum, establishing workshop approaches to writing, implementing the pedagogy of summer writing projects for teachers, tutoring younger or unskilled writers, introducing computers in composition, and publishing student writing. Reflecting interest in the reading/writing connection, thirteen products took whole or integrated language as a focus. Eight centers had reading-oriented projects growing from interests in either basic literacy or new conceptualizations of reading as process.

Origins and Development

My aim in this survey was not so much to learn about curriculum content as to discover the processes successful curriculum developers employ. Several survey items focused on how the programs originated, developed, and received approval. What needs prompted the program in the first place? Was this an outgrowth of a district or faculty decision, or, perhaps, the brainchild of one or a few people? Was it mandated by leaders other than the teachers? What sorts of procedural steps were followed in constructing the program? What stages did the development take? What approvals were necessary to implement the project?

Most respondents said that the programs were teacher-initiated. In only one case did a center originate with a school superintendent—a former English teacher with a special interest in humanities writing. One other center evolved

Figure 3.1

Planning the English Curriculum
Questionnaire on Curriculum Process

1. Please describe the general focus and content of your NCTE Centers of Excellence program (or, if available, attach a descriptive sheet or flier).

2. Describe the origins of the project. What prompted its development? How were needs identified? Was this an outgrowth of a district or faculty decision, or, perhaps, the brainchild of one or a few people?

3. What sorts of procedural steps did you follow in developing the program (e.g., curriculum review committees, board of education approval)?

4. Was any special funding required for the program? If so, what were its sources? If not, please describe how you accomplished developing the project using existing funds (or bailing wire).

5. What obstacles, problems, resistance (if any) did you have to overcome in implementing the program?

6. Please describe any particular administrative support or guidance that was helpful in program development and implementation.

7. Describe any faculty inservice or introductions to the community that were conducted as part of implementing the program.

8. What evaluation or assessment measures do you use for this program? What, in general, have been the results?

9. What plans, if any, do you have for future revisions, extensions, or developments of your program?

10. Please share any other tips, advice, or recommendations that you would offer to teachers and administrators who are engaged in curriculum planning and development.

as an outgrowth of a board of education request for stronger programs in writing; one came about when community members expressed dissatisfaction with the English language arts program. In one instance, a negative accreditation report prompted curriculum review, and in one other case, low scores on a statewide assessment spurred teachers into action. Surprisingly, only four centers were attributed to the district language arts coordinator (although coordinators were deeply involved in a much larger number of centers). It is important to note that *no* program grew from textbook adoption or review; nor did any result from external mandate for installation of a packaged program.

Forty-three of the Centers of Excellence resulted from teacher initiatives, either a single teacher or a team. Respondents emphasized that their programs worked *because* they were not mandated or imposed from the outside. According to Evelyne Berge of LaFollette High School in Madison, Wisconsin: "Our program was successful because it was teacher developed to meet the needs in our classrooms. It was not forced on us. We were allowed to determine its content and implementation. . . . It is classroom teachers who must implement; therefore they need to be developers as well."

Sharon Knipp of the Ysleta Independent School District, El Paso, Texas, summed up the sentiments of many respondents: "I would like to encourage teachers who have a vision to trust themselves and that vision, as I feel the most successful innovative programs are developed by those who know students best—the teachers."

Despite much worry about external mandates, few districts or states actually have an imposed, lock-step curriculum. The fear of mandated programs may be more of a specter than a reality. Further suspicion is cast on the stereotype of the top-down imposition when center leaders freely and gratefully acknowledged support from their school administrators. Twenty-five centers identified a building principal as a key source of support. Edith Ziegler, Lynn Stampa, and Jim Klika of the Tenakill School in Closter, New Jersey, praised their principal as "our most valuable ally. . . . He was right there to remove our own uncertainties by asking the right questions and encouraging us to build our new program."

Three schools were particularly enthusiastic about principals who had actually taken inservice training with their faculties; in two instances, principals participated in writing workshops and offered their own writings for discussion in peer group editorial sessions. Five centers identified the superintendent as a crucial source of support; five others credited the curriculum coordinator for providing the resources that were needed.

In fact, as respondents described the development of their programs, a far different sort of "mandate" emerged—a mandate, not from administrators or boards of education, but from current curriculum theory and research. The center programs clearly reflect national and international trends in English language arts instruction. As one reads the descriptions of the centers' aims, philosophies, and methodologies, one finds remarkable syntheses and consistency with emphasis on whole language, interdisciplinarity, individualized reading and response, and writing taught from a process framework.

Of course, the applicants were screened by an NCTE committee and could be expected to show up-to-date practices. Nevertheless, the consistency and coherence of the centers suggest that excellence is more than a strictly local, grassroots, teacher-initiated process. A dozen respondents mentioned the writing project movement as an important inspiration: A faculty member would attend a writing project, learn about new directions, and head back home to formulate a program. Other respondents mentioned national conferences and workshops as the impulse for program development. University courses were credited with providing fresh insights for several centers, as was reading the professional literature in English education.

The pattern of development for the Centers of Excellence seems to be a rather healthy "life cycle," wherein teachers who are in touch with national trends and issues develop grassroots applications for their classes or districts and receive support from curriculum coordinators, principals, and superintendents.

Approval Processes

Curriculum approval did not seem to present an obstacle in project development. There was virtually no evidence in the survey of stereotypical red-tape bureaucrats or myopic approval panels. Formal board of education approval was required for twelve of the programs, but none of the respondents described any particular difficulties securing this approval. Three other programs required acceptance by a district curriculum review committee, and again, no major obstacles were reported. One project simply needed the approval of an English department head, who was, in fact, a member of the planning team.

Whether the ease of approval is a causal factor for excellence in English was not clear from this survey. One needs to ask, then, whether approval was easy to obtain because the centers (and their planners) were obviously excellent or, perhaps, whether pockets of excellence are most likely to emerge in systems where the approval system is simple to negotiate. In any case, it is apparent that the primary mode of development for the centers in this sample was consensual rather than regulatory. The centers appear to be a product of agreement among teachers, administrators, and, as appropriate, the board of education, rather than an outgrowth of rule-bound procedures and processes.

Implementation

The apparent ease of approval of the Centers of Excellence may also be linked to carefully developed public information and implementation plans. Ten of the centers held workshops to explain new programs to parents. One center created a system for visits so parents could witness the new program in

25

operation. Another center even took its show on the road and made presentations to local service clubs. In addition, parental involvement in tutoring centers and writing workshops was common in the writing-oriented projects.

The importance of such public relations work was emphasized by William Anderson of the Mt. Ararat School Reading Center in Topsham, Maine: "*Every* year we have conducted workshops for faculty, given school board presentations, and/or presentations to parents. This is constant (even ten years into the program)."

The Centers of Excellence leaders spent much time and energy training and informing fellow faculty. Approaches and methods included inservice days for a department or whole faculty, use of consultants from outside the school or district, faculty meetings, and in-school workshops. Five centers emphasized the use of teachers rather than consultants as inservice leaders. Five other centers stressed the value of the National Writing Project in helping prepare faculty inservice leaders. Three centers sent at least one staff member to summer institutes, workshops, or writing projects each year to infuse fresh ideas into the program.

A literature-based program of the Albemarle County Schools in Charlottesville, Virginia, described a particularly well-developed inservice plan. Mallory Loehr reported that participating inservice teachers receive training from Albemarle County School staff and from veterans of the program during a three-day summer workshop. Other teacher leaders attend the summertime Central Virginia Writing Project. Teams of trainers are created during the school year, and frequent meetings are held throughout the year for the teacher-leaders to review their experiences.

Several center leaders also emphasized hands-on or direct learning as a form of inservice training or implementation. From the writing project movement it has become axiomatic that "writing teachers must write," and one of the most successful ways to introduce a new writing program seems to be urging and providing opportunities for fellow faculty and administrators to write and share their writing. Hands-on or direct experience is important with reading as well. A reader response program at Beaverton High School in Oregon was described by Jack Huhtala and Teresa Brandon:

> Teachers need to see themselves as readers and learners. . . . [We gather] as a department to read and discuss literature periodically in place of some department meetings. This helps us internalize the theory of reader response and understand the needs of students as they learn to discuss literature.

Virtually every center saw itself in the process of evolution. Programs were perceived as beginnings, not as final products. Plans were afoot for enlargements, extensions, and adaptations. A writing lab created for a junior high school will be extended to other buildings in one district; a writing program will be enlarged to include more literature; an integrated whole-language program for the elementary school will expand to the middle school. For the Centers of Excellence, then, implementation, public information, inservice faculty development, and future curriculum development are inextricably intertwined.

Evaluation and Assessment

The evaluation measures selected by the Centers of Excellence vary widely. Nine centers employ standardized achievement tests (most commonly the Iowa Test of Basic Skills and the Stanford Achievement Test). Three centers use state assessment data for evaluation. Two rely on ACT and SAT college aptitude scores; and two emphasize scores on Advanced Placement examinations. In total, then, sixteen centers use some form of commercial or governmental test as an evaluation tool.

An additional ten centers rely on assessment of writing samples, usually pre- and post-tests marked by the "holistic" scoring technique. Four centers report using analytic scoring of writing of the sort popularized by Educational Testing Service, with students marked on a scale that evaluates selected traits of good writing.

A host of self-evaluation tools were reported by the remaining centers. Five described external awards such as local, state, and national writing contests. Other centers used student journals, self-esteem questionnaires, self-selection into a program, college acceptances at major colleges, writing folders, editing checklists, frequency of writing use, parent feedback, and report cards. Eight centers described development of specific evaluation forms for teacher or student use. Wall charts and competency checklists were employed to monitor practices by three centers.

Predictably, most of the Centers of Excellence reported satisfaction on the parts of teachers and students. The survey did not attempt to assess the validity of the evaluation measures being employed. However, it seems important to note that virtually every center did have a well-developed evaluation scheme and that evaluation runs a full range from objective testing to highly subjective assessments.

Funding

How much does it cost to create a Center of Excellence in the English language arts? Is special funding required? If so, what are its sources?

Seventeen centers reported that "no special funding" was required to create a new program. These ranged from a full K-12 curriculum revision to the establishment of a reading center by an individual teacher. An additional six centers found financial support by redistributing funds ordinarily spent on textbooks. At the elementary level it was particularly noticeable that programs involving "real books"—library books and classroom libraries—could be funded through a faculty deciding *not* to adopt a basal reader. Two centers solicited book donations from the community. One center used a literary magazine as a fundraiser. One simply "scavenged": begging and borrowing furniture and supplies for a reading/writing center.

Five of the centers received support from existing professional development funds that were used to provide teacher released time for curriculum development. Eight programs included school support for teachers to attend summer institutes, writing projects, or university courses. And in three cases, curriculum leaders attended state-sponsored curriculum workshops. For one program, a teacher was granted a sabbatical leave to complete the necessary research.

Higher levels of funding and support were reported by four centers: One received a $33,000 state grant; one used $30,000 in district funding to create a writing lab; one received grants in unspecified amounts from local businesses and industries for summer programs; and one reported a $10,000 intermediate school district grant. Several centers described support in the form of computer hardware and software for writing/reading labs. In two of those instances, the equipment was supplied by the manufacturer as part of an educational grant.

However, the greatest number of programs were not funded at all or were developed by redistributing resources. And when extra costs were incurred, those costs were usually minimal. A summer writing project cost a school district $2,000; an outside consultant for an inservice day cost $750; a sabbatical leave drew on district funds but cost no more than the pay for a substitute teacher. Indeed, only one center leader listed a "lack of funding" as a major problem.

It is possible here to make a misleading interpretation of these findings. These results do *not* give support for a policy of "making do" on small budgets and existing monies to create new programs. Nor should the centers be held up as examples of what teachers could do if only they somehow used existing budgets more wisely. Clearly, reform in English language arts instruction need not break the bank. Still, one has to wonder about what other excellences might have happened in many of the un- or under-funded centers had a bit more money been available.

Obstacles

If funding wasn't a large problem, what were the major barriers to curriculum reform at the Centers of Excellence? In general, the survey respondents had less to say about obstacles than they did about processes, procedures, and support. These were, after all, *successful* curriculum development programs.

Among the obstacles listed, *other teachers* were listed most often. The teachers who resisted new programs were described variously as "older," afraid to abandon an existing program, convinced that a new program was mere faddism, skeptical of experimentalism, or concerned that the new program was abandoning traditional standards. In only one instance was an administrator referred to as an obstacle, and in two cases, parent objections were mentioned. (The particulars of those episodes were not reported.)

Six of the center leaders described demands on their own time as the biggest problem, leading to fatigue, occasional depression, and loss of energy. We must suspect that the underfunded, bootstrap nature of many of these programs may well have contributed to the strain on these curriculum leaders.

Advice for Curriculum Leaders

Like a good piece of writing, the curriculum projects in the Centers of Excellence have coherence, order, and structure. In addition to those elements, there is a great deal of room and respect for flexible, collegial processes. Many of the centers seem, in some respects, to have evolved rather than having been installed as packaged programs. At the same time, their growth is systematic and inspired by a clear understanding of how to get things done in human institutions.

I ended my survey with an invitation for Centers of Excellence leaders to offer tips, advice, and recommendations for other curriculum developers. I conclude this chapter with some of their suggestions:

It is important that staff and administration buy into any change in curriculum, and it is essential that teachers be well trained. Teachers who feel confident will be more likely to successfully integrate new curriculum into their classrooms.
— Harriet Schweitzer, Bartle School,
Highland Park, New Jersey

Get something started. Keep the district informed. Get other schools in the district involved. Find a money source and pay teachers for attending after school, on-site workshops.
—Jeanne Savoy and Bill Melton, Luther Burbank
Junior High School, Burbank, California

Activities should be planned to meet the specific needs of the campus, taking into account district and state requirements. Pre-made materials are not as effective.
—Kristine Riemann, Alamo Heights Junior High School,
San Antonio, Texas

Take your students out of the building once in a while. Tremendous learning can occur if we start recognizing students' real-world experiences. Respect their opinions—ask for their opinions, or they'll never learn to form them. Don't let your hidden curriculum be "only experts have trusted opinions."
—Audrey Wells, University High School,
Urbana, Illinois

Allow curriculum decisions to be made by classroom teachers. Encourage teachers to grow as professionals by trusting them. Be sure to have a curriculum leader who has vision and the ability to articulate into a significant whole all the disparate needs of the various classroom teachers and the students.
—Barry Gelsinger, Westminster High School, Westminster, Maryland

4 Four Curriculum Narratives

The previous chapter outlined some of the processes and procedures followed by schools that engage successfully in English language arts curriculum reform. This chapter illustrates the curriculum process more concretely. The following four narratives—stories, if you will—explain some of the ways specific school systems have reformed their English programs. Each narrative is written by a key person in the program's development.

The Fairbanks Writing Project

Lillian Hassler, an elementary school teacher in Fairbanks, Alaska, was deeply involved in her district's new whole-language elementary school curriculum design. The curriculum planning process included wide-scale involvement of teachers and community members, careful development of goals, and methodical implementation and assessment of results. Her narrative shows that school districts can adopt a textbook series without having texts dominate the curriculum.

The Midland Writing Network

Curriculum (r)evolution does not always lead to a formal program or curriculum guide. In the second narrative, Jan Loveless shows how a small number of language arts teachers in Midland, Michigan, became interested in the writing-as-process movement, how they educated as "pioneers" in new philosophies and techniques, and how their work eventually led to a network of teacher exchanges and inservice programs.

Her essay is of interest, too, for its discussion of change theory through a description of what can happen when a grassroots or bottom-up approach to curriculum meets with a top-down movement from a school board, even when both groups have common goals in mind.

Hampton's Language Across the Curriculum Program

Language across the curriculum is a concept that has been linked with interdisciplinary studies. Both are ideas whose times seem to be coming, with each calling for the removal of disciplinary barriers. In our third narrative, Betty Swiggett of the Hampton, Virginia, schools shows how the two ideas were developed following rather different approaches to curriculum evolution: one leading to the infusion of language instruction in many classes in the district, the other evolving into a formally articulated curriculum plan.

Houston's Project Access

Carol Kuykendall is a former director of English language arts for the Houston Independent School District and, as associate superintendent for curriculum, was one of the leaders of Project Access. This curriculum renewal process led to concurrent revisions in English, mathematics, science, and social studies. Her narrative not only shows a model process for developing a K-12 English program, but also shows that curriculum development need not—should not—result in isolation of subject matter concerns from one another.

The Fairbanks Writing Project
Lillian Hassler
Fairbanks North Star School District

In the mid-1980s teachers and administrators in Fairbanks decided to rewrite the existing curriculum to reflect process learning methods, in particular the "process" approach. The existing curriculum had been segmented with adopted texts in reading, language, and spelling. Reading texts were phonetically based with emphasis on traditional scope-and-sequence charts. But because of a shortfall in funding, curriculum reform was delayed. The Alaska State Writing Consortium continued to train Alaskan teachers in the teaching of process writing, and finally in 1986, the Fairbanks district was able to begin the task of writing a new language arts curriculum. This process was guided by Language Arts Curriculum Coordinator Marlys Henderson.

In the first year of the process, a committee was established to investigate current educational research. The committee met monthly during the school day. The committee included classroom teachers, curriculum specialists, reading teachers, representatives from the offices of Alaska Native Education and Bilingual Education, a minority representative, administrators, and parents. All grade levels and almost all schools in the district were represented. The committee took a close look at the dropout rate in the district, focusing on reaching at-risk students. The committee wanted the new curriculum to be student-centered. So, they spent the first year seeking a broad, general direction.

During that year, committee members read current research, attended professional conferences, and communicated with school districts nationwide. Marilyn Hanf Buckley, professor of education at the University of Alaska Anchorage, addressed the committee on the merits of a whole-language approach to teaching language arts. Process reading and writing were already integral parts of the teaching styles of many Fairbanks teachers. The consensus of the committee was to proceed in the direction of a whole-language curriculum.

The committee then began the work of drafting the new curriculum, meeting monthly during released time provided by the district. Subcommittees were formed to address philosophy, goals, and objectives. There was no main author of the language in the curriculum. All members of the committee, including parent representatives and representatives of the Bilingual Education Department discussed issues and reached consensus. As the work progressed, committee members reported to their colleagues and elicited feedback. In the spring of 1988, the committee presented its goals and objectives to teachers at a district inservice where teachers met in grade-level sessions with two language arts committee members acting as discussion leaders. The committee wanted to involve all teachers in review of the draft of the curriculum and to hear possible concerns, opinions, and needs of teachers.

During the summer of 1988, the committee examined possible materials for the reading part of the curriculum. The goal was to choose materials to meet curriculum needs rather than be influenced by an adopted basal reader. Pat Thurman, library and media services director, contacted publishers for possible pilot materials. A text evaluation form was created. Although it provided focus, the form was later discarded as it was considered too complex to be practical. At the end of the summer, evaluators met to select three pilot text programs.

Working closely with Nick Stayrook, director of planning and evaluation, the committee involved every school in the pilot. All three programs were placed in most schools, one grade level in each school serving as the pilot. Immediately, the project encountered a major snag when the publisher of one of the chosen series was reluctant to make materials available. The committee protested to local and regional sales representatives and, ultimately, had to contact the national sales manager. Eventually, the company supplied all materials to the district at no cost. One other publisher provided materials at fifty percent of cost. Perhaps, most important, the committee reviewed trade books along with textbook series, investigating titles chosen by librarians and the language arts committee.

During the pilot year, 1988-89, the district provided an unprecedented amount of inservicing for all teachers.

- Marilyn Buckley visited and gave inservice training to pilot teachers.
- Publishers sent people to inservice teachers using their materials.
- Joanne Yatvin, who had been a principal in a whole-language school in Wisconsin, spoke to pilot teachers.

- Jo Gusman, currently teaching in a bilingual school in California, presented whole-language techniques for use in multicultural classrooms.
- Visits were made by curriculum specialists from all over the country.
- Credit classes, taught by Fairbanks teachers, were offered through the University of Alaska Fairbanks.
- The district established the WHOLE LANGUAGE EXCHANGE NEWSLETTER, sent to every teacher.
- Voluntary whole-language exchanges were held after school once each month to give teachers philosophies, strategies, and hands-on material to use in the classroom.
- Director of Staff Development Helen Barrett secured a grant from the school district to train key people in each school to act as resource people in whole-language techniques. The teachers attended five training sessions given by Fairbanks teachers during school days.

Pilot teachers were given released time during the school day to attend many of these inservices and meetings.

There were some ongoing problems during the pilot year. Some of the pilot teachers voiced concern over the amount of time spent at meetings and the amount of extra work required. A few principals voiced an objection to the radical departure from the traditional curriculum, and some of the tradebook titles were late arriving, causing difficulty for the pilot teachers. But the committee endured, the principals cooperated, and the teachers worked very hard until the pilot was completed.

In April and May 1989 the difficult task came of completing the curriculum for school board approval. The committee spent long hours looking at all the materials and meeting with district administrators. Teacher and student activities were developed to meet goals and objectives. These activities reflected process writing and whole-language philosophies. The final curriculum was a "fleshed out" version of the overview teachers had seen in the spring of 1988.

When choosing a series for adoption, the committee first considered pre- and post-test results. The tests consisted of assessment of listening and speaking skills, direct writing assessment, and reading assessment. On the kindergarten and first grade levels, the pre- and post-test assessments were done by teacher observations. In the second through sixth grade levels, written tests prepared by the language curriculum specialists were used. These tests involved direct writing assessment using an analytical model. Other facets of the tests included multiple-choice questions and some open-ended items. A second element in determining the adopted program was a review of the education journals maintained by the pilot teachers. Lastly, the committee reviewed the proposals submitted by the publishers.

After hours of discussion, the committee agreed to recommend a literature-based, whole-language program. Before final school board approval could be secured, the committee added more specific goals to the curriculum guide, focusing on the area of correctness. These goals were included in the editing phase of the process writing strand of the curriculum.

The implementation phase was done in 1989-90 with one-third of the schools. In order to prepare teachers, parents, and the community for implementation, a whole-language symposium was held at the University of Alaska, Fairbanks. Over two hundred teachers, parents, and administrators took part. A variety of speakers presented whole-language strategies spanning the entire academic curriculum. Presentations were given by Fairbanks teachers and other speakers who were brought in from other parts of the United States and Canada. The district held a professional book fair through the week-long symposium to provide ready resource materials. A longer, three-week whole-language institute offered intensive training to twenty-eight teachers (twenty of whom were from the Fairbanks schools). The institute was held through the University of Alaska with support from the school district and the Alaska State Writing Consortium. College credit was granted for both the symposium and the institute.

Even with all the preparation and inservice, some teachers and principals were still concerned. Some teachers felt that they were not sufficiently inserviced. The Fairbanks Education Association later proposed that the school board offer an additional inservice day in December for the schools involved in implementation. Further, consultants from the purchasing publisher turned out to be less than well-versed in the whole-language approach, causing some teachers to come away from the sessions feeling that they needed more information.

During this implementation year, the language arts coordinator spent most of her time visiting schools, consulting with teachers, modeling lessons, and working with students. The WHOLE LANGUAGE EXCHANGE NEWSLETTER was still being published monthly, and the Whole Language Exchanges occurred regularly. The Fairbanks Writing Project continued to sponsor classes and speakers for teachers, administrators, and parents, and the language arts committee formed subcommittees to address teachers', administrators', and the community's concerns, which included parents' questions about the departure from the traditional phonetic-based reading program and first grade teachers' concerns that students would not be able to learn to read.

Parents, teachers, and administrators were concerned about the evaluation process. A subcommittee from the language arts committee is studying the interpretation of pre- and post-tests, and the Iowa Test of Basic skills required by the state of Alaska. Results of these standardized tests will be considered in evaluating the program, although the general feeling of educators versed in whole language is that these tests do not accurately reflect student achievement. This evaluation subcommittee is also reviewing the current school district report cards to see what changes need to be made to reflect the new curriculum.

Some other concerns being addressed by subcommittees are the need for a spelling handbook, the recognized need for a balanced reading program, the question of whether there should be a list of "sacred" books for use on specific grade levels, and the use of a reading workshop approach.

The Fairbanks North Star Borough School District has committed itself and its teachers to the new curriculum. Credit classes for teachers will continue, and the district has started a professional book club to make resources more available to staff. The whole-language institute and symposium will continue on an even larger scale.

As a classroom teacher who has used literature-based reading for three years, this new curriculum both excites and frightens me. As I meet people and travel to professional conferences during this sabbatical year, I find the Fairbanks curriculum constantly validated by experts in the field of language arts. Current educational research overwhelmingly supports the direction we have taken. But more than this, I have seen in my own students a new love of reading and a new fluency in writing and speaking. This is especially exciting in the multicultural classroom. Whole language allows for more flexibility in the teaching of bilingual students. It offers new methods for reaching at-risk students. But change as essential as this takes time. The educational community, as a whole, must be patient. Teachers must wean themselves from their manuals and become confident in this new empowerment. Universities must make training available for educators. The success of the student is always the first priority, but parents must be patient, for results won't be immediately measurable. We have taken on this challenge in Fairbanks, and I am confident that we have the commitment to see it through to a successful conclusion and a better way of learning language for all our students.

The Midland Writing Network
Jan Loveless
Midland, Michigan, Public Schools

I recently moved to a California corporate education position from an administrative post in the Midland, Michigan, public schools, where I taught English for eight years. A few weeks into my new job, I heard the training manager speak on the topic of change. He defined it as "a planned or unplanned response of an organization to pressure; a state of mind; an attitude." I immediately thought of Midland and the revolution in the language arts curriculum I witnessed between 1984 and 1989. Were those changes a response to pressure? Yes, I decided, they were—though the pressure was often positive, and it often came from within the system. Were all the changes planned? No. I'm convinced that no one involved could have foreseen what would happen if we began to investigate teaching writing as a process.

Clearly, Midland plans carefully for change. The Curriculum Council, a standing committee of citizens, teachers, students, and administrators, led by the director of curriculum, begins each year by inviting research suggestions from the community and the school system. When it is through studying a topic, the Curriculum Council often suggests that the board of education consider curriculum change.

Three other avenues for change—Major Change Proposals, Summer Study Proposals, and Text Study Proposals—can be initiated by any teacher or administrator. In addition, the elementary curriculum changes systematically through regularly scheduled text adoptions and concurrent rethinking of programs.

The key question, though, is, what inspires a rethinking? What creates the atmosphere that generates change? In other words, how does change "pressure" build? I think partial answers are suggested by the works of two writers outside the traditional province of public education. In 1985, Joel Barker, a process futurist, wrote *Discovering the Future: The Business of Paradigms* to build on the ideas of Thomas S. Kuhn, a scientific historian who described paradigm shifts in *The Structure of Scientific Revolution* (Kuhn 1962). Focusing on the realm of business, Barker defines a paradigm as a set of rules for success in a particular game. It defines the boundaries of the playing field and tells a player how to win within those boundaries. A paradigm shift, according to Barker (1988), "is a change to a new game, a new set of rules." It occurs when some critical mass of problems can't be solved by the old rules, and someone creative, often a neophyte player, invents a new game. That is, it happens when sufficient pressure develops and somebody responds to it by changing.

Hold that thought, and consider the ideas of James Gleick (1987), author of *Chaos: Making A New Science*. In one chapter, Gleick examines "The Butterfly Effect" in meteorology—the dramatic long-term impact of a single randomly occurring event on the weather. Without such events, which happen constantly and seemingly chaotically, Gleick explains, this planet's weather would be perfectly predictable.

Now, consider the pressure for change that developed in Midland after Judy Isquith became coordinator of language arts in 1983. Though the resulting events may not seem "randomly occurring" when viewed in retrospect, their cumulative effect was much more extensive than Isquith could have predicted.

In November 1983, Isquith asked the English teachers of both Midland high schools if they were interested in improving writing at the secondary level. When several teachers answered "yes," Isquith created a group that first called itself the Writing Across the Curriculum Committee, and eventually became known as the Midland County Writing Network. The group decided there was a need for consciousness-raising, so they invited two "thought provokers" to town in the spring of 1984. One was Sheila Fitzgerald, co-chair of a National Council of Teachers of English Committee on Strategies for Improving Language and Literacy Instruction and professor at Michigan State University's Department of Teacher Education. She spoke to teachers in kindergarten through eighth grade. Another key consultant was Art Young, the architect of Michigan Technological University's nationally respected writing across the curriculum program, who addressed seventh through twelfth grade teachers.

The speakers piqued so much interest that the Writing Network began to look for summer inservice leaders. They invited Young back to conduct a week-long workshop on writing across the curriculum for secondary teachers. For K-8 teachers, the Network invited Nancie Atwell, intermediate teacher and director of the Boothbay Writing Project, Boothbay Harbor, Maine.

The summer inservice took effect in Midland demonstrably, but gradually. Teachers who attended were excited and nervous about the ideas they'd heard, a startlingly different set of rules for playing the teaching-of-writing game. Letting kids choose their own topics? Portfolio grading? Evaluation conferences? Writing in mathematics classes? These ideas seemed pretty radical to many Midland educators. Despite some reservations and unanswered questions, in the fall of 1984, a small group of teachers began to try some of the approaches suggested by these speakers and they became enthusiastic about the results. Through informal sharing in department offices, cafeterias, hallways, and lounges, they motivated other teachers to experiment with the new ways or at least to attend the next Network-sponsored workshop.

Meanwhile, the Midland County Writing Network began to publish "The Write Stuff," a newsletter that shared tips on teaching writing. Editor Martha Briggs was a great proponent of writing across the curriculum; she made sure the newsletter informed its readers of content-area teachers' successes with writing as a learning tool.

Then, as part of its regularly scheduled adoption process, the standing elementary language arts committee began to examine the language arts curriculum K-6. Their initial survey indicated that little writing was going on in elementary classrooms. They resolved to change that situation and began to meet regularly, reading research and sharing information. They went far beyond a mere textbook adoption to the creation of a language arts philosophy for elementary schools. The curriculum that emerged and was finally adopted in 1986 was much more a whole-language than a textbook-driven approach.

At the secondary level, the process of change moved more slowly. It was connected to the elementary movement only through the involvement of Isquith and the few secondary teachers who were attending network meetings. These teachers were examining writing in the content areas and writing across the curriculum. Briggs and Jan Goodall, both high school English teachers, began a buddy system to trade writing ideas with teachers of other subjects. Several of their converts began to attend network meetings and to rethink their beliefs about instruction.

Responding to requests for inservice, the Writing Network sponsored a second set of summer workshops in 1985. Robert Jones of Michigan Tech led a writing-in-the-content-areas workshop for secondary teachers. The elementary workshop leader was Shelley Harwayne, assistant director of the New York City Staff Development Writing Process Project. The Project, directed by Lucy McCormick Calkins, was a joint effort between Teachers College, Columbia University, and the New York City Schools. Harwayne's workshop motivated elementary teachers Hilary Ferguson and Judy Zak and me (a seventh grade teacher) to request permission to go to New York City to observe the Staff Development Project firsthand.

Our promise was that we would bring some of the essence of the Writing Process Project back to Midland. We would share what we learned through workshops with other teachers. A great benefit of the trip proved to be confirmation of the paradigm shift we and others in Midland were making in our thinking. New York was not yet using a writing process approach in secondary schools, but their elementary program was fairly similar to the work Ferguson and Zak were already doing. That affirmation was a great morale boost to us all, and I was convinced that a process approach to writing would work in secondary classrooms. We three came home resolved to do more sharing, to continue experimenting with a workshop atmosphere in our classrooms, and to have our students write for one another.

In the spring of 1986, we New York travelers launched the "Big Book Project." My seventh graders created oversized books with large print (as recommended by Don Holdaway) for Ferguson's kindergartners. The pride of authorship of the seventh graders and the responsive joy of the kindergartners sold us completely on cross-grade publishing and on the impact of writing for real audiences. Other teachers, impressed with our success, have since instituted many other opportunities for cross-grade or cross-age-span publishing. Now Midland High School students even adopt "grandparents" at a local retirement home and write for them. Publishing, we've learned, can take a variety of forms.

By fall of 1986, Ferguson and Zak had established a regular sharing group similar in collegiality and influence to the sessions we had observed in New York City. The Midland group, dubbed "Between the Lines," proved to be the impetus many elementary teachers needed to keep pioneering the new paradigm.

Also in the fall of 1986, we hosted an evening workshop for teachers interested in learning more about the process approach to teaching writing. The program was well attended; our audience included a few teachers who had previously been hostile to the new ideas. I thought of the folk wisdom I'd heard once: An old head needs nine exposures to a new idea before the concept "takes." Some of our audience had had at least seven exposures, and the paradigm was beginning to germinate in their thoughts.

At this point, independent events helped our cause. Larry Levy, a member of the English department of a local college, was elected to the school board. He was eager to institute a district writing policy like the successful one in the Alma, Michigan schools. Meanwhile, several parents of intermediate students began to complain about a lack of challenge in the intermediate curriculum, and some teachers who had tried the workshop approach to teaching writing began to express discomfort about the standard practice of relying on worksheets in remedial classes. This dissatisfaction with the status quo spawned fertile discussions in meetings of the Intermediate School English Committee.

The committee, a standing group whose purpose was to examine and communicate about curriculum and instruction, convened in 1986 to undertake a major study of the intermediate English curriculum. It began with a survey to find out how the intermediate program was serving its customers—the current students, the parents, the high school English teachers, and the high school students who'd been through it. The survey results showed a strong desire for change on everyone's part. The committee then began an examination of the research literature about intermediate English, which continues today.

Other events that fueled the efforts of Midland's paradigm pioneers included the publication of two critical documents—the state Department of Education and Michigan Council of Teachers of English joint compilation of *Michigan Essential Goals and Objectives for Writing* (DOE and MCTE 1985) and the Department of Education's *The State Plan and Position Statement on Writing Education* (DOE 1987). Also helpful was Michigan's newly adopted definition of reading as "interaction between reader and text." All these official stances supported the teaching of language as a process.

During the summer of 1986, the Writing Network again hosted inservice training. The secondary workshop on writing across the curriculum was team taught by Robert Jones and Midland's own Briggs. Martha Horn, a teacher trainer in the Teachers College Writing Project, worked with the elementary teachers. She asked that children be present for her workshop, then dazzled participants with a magical demonstration of teaching kids she'd never seen before. The workshop participants asked the Writing Network to bring Horn back during the school year. She conducted a week-long evening workshop in the fall of 1987, then returned in February 1988 to do demonstration teaching in Midland classrooms as a follow-up for the fall participants. Each workshop added to the number of Midland teachers experimenting with the new paradigm.

By fall of 1987, the school board had divided itself into "Knowledge Centers," small groups of board members who researched certain topics. The Curriculum Knowledge Center lunched with Isquith, Jan Goodall (former language department head of H. H. Dow High School), and me (at that time I was language department head of H. H. Dow High). Representatives from the lower grades and area colleges also joined the luncheon. The board members wanted our opinions of how things were going in language arts. One lunch led to several more meetings, and eventually the board asked Isquith and me to draft a district writing policy. The document went through multiple considerations and revisions that fall and spring. The school board adopted the final revision in July of 1988.

The adoption of this policy sparked controversy, both among secondary content-area teachers who felt threatened by the idea of a writing mandate, and among paradigm pioneers who felt their bottom-up efforts at change had been working slowly but well without interference. Fear and anger, the instant reaction of many teachers to the writing policy, were fueled for a time by rumors and misconceptions. A number of content-area teachers thought they would have to add "teaching English" to their already demanding assignments. Others resented a quotation from *Michigan Essential Goals and Objectives for Writing* that described worksheets, blank-filling exercises, and multiple-choice tests as techniques to "avoid having students write." A third group resented any document that seemed to impugn their expertise as instructional designers.

In response to this negative reaction, Briggs and both high school English department heads conducted a series of more than twenty after-school policy explanation inservices for the entire Midland Public Schools secondary staff. Isquith met with the faculties of all elementary schools to provide the same inservice. Most teachers left these sessions with a better understanding of writing as a learning strategy they could incorporate into other subjects. They also understood more fully that the policy was an endorsement of the state's position on writing as a means of "self-expression, discovery, and critical thinking." Finally, they began to comprehend that using writing in their classes would not necessarily add to their workload. They would not be expected to teach English.

As their fears dissipated, teachers grew more comfortable with the writing policy. While the jury is still out on top-down versus bottom-up change, the board's adoption of the writing policy has already had the positive effect of getting teachers of different disciplines to talk to each other and think about what they have in common.

The summer of 1988 saw still more writing inservices, this time led by home-grown experts. Ferguson and Zak conducted a very successful workshop for elementary teachers, and Briggs led a writing-to-learn workshop for secondary teachers. Inservice participants from the Intermediate School English Committee returned eager to continue their work on the new curriculum, which went into effect in the fall of 1990. Although I moved to California in July of 1989, I know that Ferguson and Zak conducted two workshops for elementary teachers in the summer of 1990. Linda Reif, a seventh and eighth grade teacher, led a very successful workshop for the intermediate school English teachers. Many of the participants are now beginning to implement the new paradigm.

Feeling the change pressure from the lower grades and the obvious enthusiasm for the new paradigm displayed by pioneers, the high school teachers in Midland are now beginning to question the appropriateness of their twenty-year-old curriculum. As I left H. H. Dow High School, teachers were just launching a major rethinking effort that continues today.

Another professional developmental approach that continues in Midland is what Japanese managers call "nemawashee": discussing, sharing, and listening. We held Reading-Writing Days at the mall to demonstrate writing as a process to elementary students and their parents. We conducted Young Authors' Teas and Conferences. We invited parents into our classrooms. We attended and spoke at professional conferences. We took courses from exciting thinkers at colleges around the area. Kay Harley, a professor at Saginaw Valley State University who returned in 1988 from a sabbatical in Australia, interested us in her action research class and became our sponsor for several colloquiums and publications. John Dinan and Bob Root of Central Michigan University devoted an entire issue of the *Language Arts Journal of Michigan* to the research reports that sprang from Kay's class. Stephen Tchudi and Marilyn Wilson, professors of English Education at Michigan State University, offered a year-long seminar that required action research and documentation of results.

Although I've left out hundreds of influential conversations among teachers and hosts of other "butterflies," I hope I've shown the very real effect of their occurrence in Midland. Elementary teachers and intermediate teachers have continued to study and revise their curriculums. The high school English teachers are beginning to examine theirs, and the whole system is experiencing the energizing aftermath of a paradigm shift. Our examination of writing has led us much further than we thought we would go. We are now seeing all effective teaching and learning as something quite different from the presentational model we grew up with.

The effects of our work are now easy to recognize. For example, the district is considering ongoing financial support through a line budget for the Midland County Writing Network. Isquith tells me that recently, the Midland teachers attended a seminar on collaborative learning and came back ready to factor these ideas into the program. The superintendent, the coordinator of science, and an elementary teacher spent a week at the National Science Resources Center in Washington, D.C. There they learned about exciting units that they brought back to pilot. Now elementary students are studying science hands-on, and writing reams of reading/writing journal pages about what they learn. Through a new science resources center, teachers in the entire county are learing how to integrate elementary curriculums in experiential, project-based teaching that incorporates the latest research on collaborative learning, critical thinking, and "languaging."

The Midland Public Schools curriculum change process has been, as Isquith admits, "messy." Real curriculum change is not neat, the way they tell you in curriculum books. It happens because the weight of dissatisfaction with an existing approach inspires someone to change the rules of the game. The paradigm shifter enlists followers—the paradigm pioneers of Joel Barker's book. And finally, the evidence that the new method works convinces others to change. Midland hasn't completed this last stage yet, but it's getting there.

Formal change, the business of proposals and recommendations, is ultimately driven by attitude, by mindset, by the informal changes that come about because somebody's been exposed to a new idea, has gotten excited about it, and has gone forth to spread it. Curriculum change defies lock-step planning because each new concept affects and helps generate others. Change happens because of new ideas, curriculum leaders who research, a receptive school board and superintendent, innovative teachers—and, of course, the Butterfly Effect.

Using Language for Learning Across the Curriculum

Betty Swiggett
Hampton, Virginia, City Schools

The Hampton, Virginia, school system has given strong support to the integration of the language processes with content learning. First, in 1984, the Hampton schools developed a middle school interdisciplinary core curriculum, and then, in 1985, they developed a plan for writing across the curriculum. Today there are several major interdisciplinary programs in place: core academic programs for grades four through eight (social studies, language arts, mathematics, and science); remediation programs for at-risk students; and gifted programs for grades one through twelve. The writing across the curriculum project has merged with the interdisciplinary programs described above, but it has also retained a thrust of its own because of its broad focus on writing as a tool for learning in all disciplines.

The planning processes for the interdisciplinary programs and the writing across the curriculum program were decidedly different. The interdisciplinary curriculum involved specific units for specific age groups and required intensive curriculum planning using interdisciplinary teams. The writing across the curriculum project was approached as non-programmatically as possible. It is a "metacurriculum," one that presents strategies that can be applied in flexible ways by classroom teachers to any content area. Curriculum leaders in Hampton learned much of what they know about successful implementation of language across the curriculum through the middle school interdisciplinary curriculum and the writing across the curriculum projects.

Planning a Middle School Interdisciplinary Curriculum

At the beginning of the 1983-84 school year the Hampton school board approved and provided the financial support for change from a junior high school structure to a middle school design. The new organization would pay attention to balancing the humane and academic elements of schooling— bridging the gap between the self-contained elementary classroom and the fully departmentalized schedule of the high school day.

Middle school literature (ASCD 1975, Lounsburg and Vars 1978, Merebloom 1983, NMSA 1982) consistently recommends interdisciplinary approaches to instruction. Therefore, it was decided that in our middle school plan students would be assigned for their core academic program to interdisciplinary teams of teachers. These teams would be responsible also for developmental reading instruction and a program that focused on interpersonal skills, decision-making abilities, and goal setting. Students would leave the core team setting for physical education and elective/exploratory courses. During the two blocks of time that students were away, teachers would be involved in team and individual planning for instruction. The plan was to operate middle schools for the first two years with only seventh and eighth graders enrolled in the program, after which sixth graders would be enrolled.

Forming a Curriculum Leadership Team

With the general organizational design of the middle school program needing only refinement, attention turned to curriculum designs for local programs. In Hampton, the understanding of interdisciplinary instruction among committee members and others did not run deep. Teachers had seen no model interdisciplinary programs in their visits to other school divisions. Further, when they left the rarified atmosphere of workshops on middle school organization and programs, they returned to the departmentalized junior high school setting, which provided them few opportunities to work closely with teachers of other subjects.

Allen L. Davis III, assistant superintendent of secondary education and instructional services, decided that the best way to begin the transition to a middle school system would be to form a leadership team composed of the core curriculum specialists and the reading specialist. Not only did these curriculum specialists have a long, established, and warm working relationship with each other, but they also knew all the teachers in the core subjects and understood their concerns.

Davis conferred with Stephen Tchudi, author of this book and then president of the National Council of Teachers of English, who was a consultant to the school system in the preparation and implementation of a developmental English program, grades seven through twelve. Tchudi had begun talking with English teachers about making English instruction interdisciplinary. That same semester, Tchudi was experiencing, firsthand, interdisciplinary team teaching of seventh graders in a language arts/social studies block in a Michigan public school. His affirmation of the benefits of interdisciplinary instruction for middle schoolers provided Davis the encouragement he needed to proceed with curriculum development without delay. Because of my experience in curriculum development and previous work with interdisciplinary projects on a smaller scale, I was appointed to chair the interdisciplinary curriculum project.

Curriculum planning occurred in two principal stages: (1) the development of an interdisciplinary planning process with related inservice sessions for administrators and teachers, and (2) writing of curriculum by teams of teachers under the guidance of the curriculum specialists.

Developing a Planning Process

The curriculum specialists in English, social studies, mathematics, science, and reading, along with the director of library/media services, reviewed the existing curriculum guides, objective by objective, and were impressed with the strong focus on learning processes in all areas. They organized "process strands" across disciplines into major categories:

- working with others
- locating, acquiring, and organizing information
- expanding vocabulary
- evaluating/problem solving
- communicating orally and in writing
- using technology

Central to each of these processes is language, its use and development. These shared process objectives became the starting point for curriculum workshops.

The leadership team saw the need to capture the important ideas and processes that they used in thinking through interdisciplinary curriculum development and thus created a handbook for teachers: *A Guide for Team Planning*. This guide contains a rationale for interdisciplinary instruction, guidelines for effective team membership, suggestions on approaching learning as a process, and a complete correlation of shared objectives across the four core areas, reading, and library instruction. The guide also contains sample interdisciplinary units, a list of resources, and worksheets for team planning.

As the leadership team reflected on approaches to interdisciplinary instruction, the members became convinced that reading should be integrated naturally into the interdisciplinary curriculum. They recommended that reading instruction be built into the core academic program, but the members of the Middle School Steering Committee were not receptive. They favored the integration of reading into the content areas but not at the expense of losing a separate course, so they rejected the proposal. Some six years later, the thinking changed and principals and teachers began taking steps to integrate reading into the core interdisciplinary program.

Introducing Interdisciplinary Planning to Teachers

Just prior to the opening of schools in 1984, the curriculum leadership team conducted an all-day interdisciplinary planning workshop for the core academic teachers at grades seven and eight. The leadership team wanted to initiate curriculum development by having teams generate their own units and correlated activities. Principals had already organized teachers into interdisciplinary teams in anticipation of the shift to the middle school plan. Working with their own team members, teachers began the interdisciplinary planning process. By the end of the day, several teams had outlined short, workable units appropriate for use during the first quarter. One group, for example, outlined activities in social studies, science, and mathematics to support the students' study of mythology in English classes. Topics to be explored included the influence of mythology on landforms and place names, scientific explanations of superstitions, and ancient numeration systems. These teams were the exceptions, however. Most teachers revealed a need for a much more thorough orientation to interdisciplinary planning.

The core curriculum specialists therefore developed a series of four all-day curriculum writing workshops spread over four months. Teachers were drawn from all five junior high schools and organized into four-member interdisciplinary teams, with persons on each team drawn from four different schools. *A Guide for Team Planning* was used as a resource for developing curriculum units. By May 1985 teachers had learned to work as team members and had produced curriculums to be used the following school year.

All units reflected six principles for developing interdisciplinary instruction: (1) a focus on broad themes and issues; (2) strong subject content; (3) creation of multiple perspectives on experience; (4) integration and correlation of learning, both in processes and content; (5) activities that accommodate different learning rates, styles, and interests; and (6) a focus on learning by doing.

As curriculum writing progressed, participants became aware that although excellent interdisciplinary themes could originate from the content of any discipline, social studies consistently provided an ideal framework for developing rich thematic units because it dealt with people, places, and events in various cultural settings. Therefore, in 1986, when the division began its next interdisciplinary curriculum projects—the sixth grade curriculum and the elementary school-based gifted curriculum—social studies topics became the framework for writing comprehensive thematic units.

Implementation and Evaluation

The core curriculum specialists took on the responsibility of mentoring the program through the initial implementation stage. Besides the usual oreintation workshops, visitations, consultations, and provisions of resources, the specialists arranged for interdisciplinary curriculum-based field trips for the classes. The first was a trip to Mariners' Museum in nearby Newport News, which complemented the seventh grade student-as-scientist unit. Students experienced hands-on inquiry/discovery activities related to sea life. These experiences provided students with new ideas for scientific projects and demonstrated the interdisciplinary nature of real-life activities. Currently, students in grades four through eight have at least one field trip arranged at the division level per year to support interdisciplinary curriculum.

To give recognition to the students for their hard work and acquaint the general public with the new curriculum, the planners arranged for a public display of student interdisciplinary projects at a large shopping mall during Hampton Education Week. This encouraged the preparation of attractive displays by many teams, creating a cooperative climate in which students and teachers learned from one another.

In October 1985 representatives of the interdisciplinary teams met with the curriculum specialists to review the progress of curriculum implementation. The meeting served to answer many questions of the nuts-and-bolts variety and to affirm that the curriculum was flexible but not optional. It revealed also that teachers were experiencing growing pains in human relations, which is inherent in the team-building process. The representatives asked that additional staff development be offered in team teaching and interdisciplinary instruction. Curriculum specialists and school administrators continue to provide assistance through workshops, college courses, and various other resources. In the spring of 1986 the original writing teams reconvened to review and make modifications in the guides as required. Because the guides had undergone two revisions during the workshop period, no major changes were needed.

Teachers and students are the final evaluators of the success of any new curriculum. In reflecting upon the effects of the interdisciplinary approach on herself and her students, one teacher-writer who participated in the fourth thorugh sixth grade curriculum development said: "I underwent a metamorphosis when I participated in the interdisciplinary curriculum writing project. The experience lit a fire under a burnt-out teacher. Any teacher who uses the curriculum for one semester will not stop. I have found interdisciplinary approaches more efficient than other approaches. The best part, however, is the students' enthusiasm. Students will have it no other way."

Writing Across the Curriculum, K-12

In the spring of 1985, the school division incorporated into its new long-range plan an objective to implement a writing across the curriculum program, K-12. As the English curriculum specialist for the division, I was assigned primary responsibility for overseeing program implementation.

Although my supervisory plate was full, I could not shirk responsibility for this objective. I inquired about the committee deliberations that led to the selection of this "revolutionary" direction. Planning committee members explained that it was the desire of the committee to change the perception of writing from something done in elementary language arts lessons and secondary English classes to an activity appropriate for use in all content areas. Politically sensitive, the planning committee was responding to the public call for improved student writing. Writing reform efforts, particularly the writing across the curriculum movement, offered strategies that could be applied divisionwide.

Forming a Steering Committee

The first need, obviously, was to change the image of the program from an English project to a school division project. Therefore, my first step in getting the program underway was to form a steering committee with broad representation from the elementary and secondary levels. To assist in orienting committee members to the essential concepts of effective writing across the curriculum programs, I invited Stephen and Susan Tchudi to conduct an all-day workshop. The committee was enlarged for this session to include teachers from every school in the division.

The Tchudis converted language and learning theory into very practical classroom writing activities. They advocated a focus on workaday writing—for example, active notetaking, keeping learning logs, summarizing learning on 3 x 5 cards, and writing class newsletters to parents. Workshop participants gained a better understanding of the concept of writing as a tool for learning and as a strategy that required no more time than other teaching techniques. The Tchudis offered four important recommendations for program design:

1. Define the program as a writing-to-learn program, thereby shifting the primary concern from the quality of writing to a means of improving content learning.

2. Take a "non-program" approach. Writing should not be viewed as an add-on activity. It is a technique for thinking and learning.

3. Build the teachers' confidence that they already have some strategies in place; enhance current practices to increase composition at all levels; and persuade teachers that writing is a highly productive activity for learning.

4. Provide inservice for all levels of instructional leadership—long-range planning committees, administrators, and classroom teachers.

Developing an Implementation Plan

The steering committee devoted its first year to needs assessment and the development of an implementation plan. The committee conducted approximately 150 interviews of teachers, students, administrators, and parents regarding the types of writing done in school and perceptions about the value of writing. The survey revealed that although teachers and students used writing-to-learn strategies to varying degrees, the principal emphasis was on written products—creative writing at the elementary level and essay writing at the secondary level. Writing took place most often in English and social studies classes, least often in mathematics and physical education classes. Students said that the writing activities that brought the most learning were those tied to doing research—activities that required strong student ownership of learning. The survey was convincing evidence of the need to improve teachers' understanding of the numerous ways that writing can serve as a tool for learning in every subject.

The Steering Committee's approach to implementing writing-to-learn strategies across the curriculum contained three primary elements:

1. A writing-to-learn handbook for teachers, K-12. The handbook, written by teachers and curriculum specialists, is a compact document that presents writing-to-learn activities for each content area for the various stages of the learning process: introductory, during the lesson, and following the lesson.

2. Writing-to-learn presentations/workshops for administrators and teachers. The steering committee sponsored several inservice opportunities. In researching the literature on writing across the curriculum in preparation for conducting workshops, the steering committee continually returned to Shirley Haley-James' (1982) article, "Helping Students Learn Through Writing," for its succinct statements on how writing encourages learning. Fortunately, there were three expert teachers on the steering committee, fellows of the Eastern Virginia Writing Project, who could illustrate the benefits of writing to learn with samples of student work from their own classrooms. Every teacher received a copy of the writing-to-learn handbook. Workshops were conducted the following fall for principals, core academic secondary teachers, and all elementary teachers, the latter in grade level groups.

3. The publication of a newsletter. To keep teacher dialogue active, the steering committee decided to publish a semi-annual newsletter. *The Write Connections* provides teachers a medium for sharing effective writing-to-learn strategies. It does several other things as well: it contains personal accounts by teachers of how they came to understand the value of writing to learn; it gives top administrators a medium for writing about their own composing processes; and, as the one instructional publication that every teacher in the school system receives, it keeps the division's focus on writing to learn in the forefront of teachers' thoughts.

Effectiveness of the Plan

At this writing, there is much evidence of success in the writing to learn across the curriculum program. First, there is broad acceptance on the part of teachers and administrators of the value of writing in all content areas, something that could not have been achieved without a divisionwide emphasis. Second, as teachers have come to see ways to use writing for learning without the onus of grading, more writing has occurred. Third, in schools and departments where at least one teacher is a strong advocate of writing to learn, the whole group uses strategies more consistently.

Other influences have merged with the writing-to-learn emphasis to increase the use of writing in the content areas. The new Virginia Standards of Learning Objectives for Language Arts require that a process approach to the teaching of writing begin in the primary grades. To help teachers meet this new objective, an elementary writing guide that contains both writing-to-learn activities and a writing-process approach has been developed. Writing workshops were conducted in the fall of 1989 to introduce the new writing guide to teachers. As teachers deepened their knowledge of the developmental stages of writing, many began to understand that writing need not wait for specific skills development—it can begin the first day of school.

Equally important is the fact that the interdisciplinary approach, which began at the middle school level, has become the primary curricular approach at the elementary level in every type of program—for gifted, regular, and at-risk students.

As a school system, we have come to appreciate the central role that language plays in all subjects in making meaning out of the flux of experience, and the special role that writing plays in developing complex thoughts and preserving them for further examination.

Project ACCESS
Carol Kuykendall
Houston Independent School District

Any account of curriculum renewal in Houston, Texas, must begin with Joan Raymond, the general superintendent who has made curriculum a cornerstone of her administration and trusted development of that curriculum to teachers.

"We are going to approach the development of curriculum in this district as if there is *no* curriculum."

With these words, Raymond issued a challenge without precedent in the Houston Independent School District (HISD). The mandate was to move beyond patchwork attempts at improving curriculum piece-by-piece and to undertake nothing less than a complete rethinking of the whole. Furthermore, the rethinking was to be done by those closest to Houston's 190,000+ students—the city's almost 11,000 teachers. On this point, Raymond left no doubt: "This is going to be a totally teacher-developed, teacher-managed, teacher-controlled, teacher-evaluated curriculum. . . . That is the only way it will work. Teachers have got to own it."

In the spring of 1987, when an accreditation team of the Texas Education Agency identified curriculum guides as one of twenty-three areas requiring corrective action by the district, Raymond chose to go far beyond the minimal improvements required. Indeed, she set in motion a process for rethinking the entire K-12 curriculum. Her plan, presented at a districtwide meeting of principals in late September 1987, called for the principals of each elementary school to identify that school's most outstanding teacher. Middle and high school principals were to identify their schools' best teachers in each of four content areas—English language arts, mathematics, science, and social studies.

The teachers identified by principals across the city would comprise the curriculum advisory committee, which would immediately begin to study the existing curriculum and to develop guidelines for change. As soon as possible after the beginning of the second semester, fifty of these teachers would be relieved of classroom duty for full-time work on curriculum guides. These writers would be chosen on the basis of grade levels selected as priorities for the first year of the project. At the beginning of the next school year, the teachers would return to their home schools and be replaced by teachers who had been selected to write guides for other levels according to a master plan developed by the advisory committee. This process would be repeated each year until all curriculum guides for core subjects had been completed.

As assistant superintendent for curriculum in Houston schools, I listened to this plan with a great deal of interest. I kept thinking of an adage we all heard as children: Be careful what you want; you just might get it. At least hypothetically, here was what we *all* wanted—a veritable blank check to develop curriculum as it should be developed. The challenge of creating a model for such a mega-project seemed staggering.

My mental arithmetic worked well enough to raise a red flag about the size of that curriculum advisory committee. Given one member for each of Houston's approximately 170 elementary schools and four members for each of its 37 middle schools and 26 high schools, the committee was bound to be large—well over 400 educators. If we chose to add representatives of such elective areas as fine arts, physical education, and foreign languages as well as a few computer teachers and librarians, the total would exceed 450. How could we organize such an unwieldy group to do thoughtful, substantive work? Where could we meet? Perhaps most important, how could those of us charged with providing leadership do so while making sure that teachers were really in charge of decision making?

What follows is an account of how we dealt—and continue to deal—with such questions. As a long-time teacher and former director of English language arts in HISD, I was especially interested in the development of curriculum in my own content area. Given the focus of this ASCD monograph, I will draw my illustrations from Houston's new language arts curriculum, even while emphasizing that parallel developments were—and are—taking place across the curriculum. It should be noted that this account is written *in medias res*. We offer a model for grassroots curriculum development in a major urban district, but it is a model that continues to evolve. The more we learn, the more we realize remains to be learned.

Forging a Common Vision

Dubbing Houston's curriculum development effort Project ACCESS was no casual decision. To many of us who chose to work in the nation's sixth largest school system, this acronym captures the fundamental challenge: Making all learning accessible to all students. At present, the students served in Houston's schools are 41 percent black, 41 percent hispanic, 16 percent anglo, 3 percent Asian, and slightly under 1 percent American Indian. More than half come from families with incomes so low that the children qualify for free or reduced lunches. The remainder range from borderline poverty to great affluence. More than 16 percent of students served by Houston's schools have limited proficiency in English while still others enter kindergarten already beginning to read and write. Aspirations and levels of achievement are equally as diverse. These students—*all* of these students—are targeted in the acronym Project ACCESS: A Collaborative Curriculum to Enhance Student Success.

During the first phase of the project, the curriculum advisory committee's work was organized around four Saturday work sessions, spaced to allow

51

preparatory and follow-up activities on individual campuses. Each day began with an opening general session, usually featuring remarks by General Superintendent Raymond and an overview of the work to follow. The work was accomplished in small groups facilitated by teachers who had developed task packets used to structure activities leading to committee recommendations. These recommendations were then distributed to schools, where committee representatives shared them with colleagues for consideration and response. Suggestions for change were then collected from each campus and incorporated into revised sets of recommendations that would lay the foundation for subsequent deliberations and development of new curriculum guides.

The first session focused on overarching curriculum issues across the disciplines followed by statements framed by each curriculum area. Concerned that all high school graduates be able to use language successfully, the English group crystallized its consensus as follows:

> Our integrated language arts curriculum centers on the child, focuses on literature, and anticipates the future. Students will develop a sense of identity and explore relationships with others and the physical world while becoming independent thinkers and effective communicators.

The second session focused on the needs of learners at various developmental levels. How can curriculum help teachers accommodate the needs of students with a wide range of abilities, backgrounds, interests, and ways of learning? How can it help teachers provide learning experiences appropriate for students at different stages of growth? How do young people learn best at each of those stages? By working through a series of individual and small-group activities, the committee developed consensus lists of answers to these questions. Although these specifications cut across all content areas, they later helped English teachers make hard decisions about when to begin teaching what and how.

During its third work session, the curriculum advisory committee began to focus explicitly on issues of content. In preparation for this session, each elementary teacher was assigned, according to background and preference, to one of the core subject areas already represented by departmentalized middle and high school teachers. Resource packets distributed in preparation for this session were differentiated by content area. All included state curriculum frameworks as well as curriculum recommendations by national subject-area associations.

Here, I must confess disappointment that the NCTE—unlike its counterparts in mathematics, science, and social studies—offers no recommended framework for curriculum change. In preparing for their work sessions, English teachers had to glean what they could from NCTE's most recent edition of *Recommended English Language Arts Curriculum Guides, K-12* and excerpts from the 1982 publication *Essentials of English*. They were also encouraged to review journal articles and professional books focusing on curriculum trends of promising models for the teaching of language arts.

This third work session of the curriculum advisory committee presented a formidable challenge: Within a few hours, each subcommittee was to shape the beginnings of a K-12 framework for curriculum in a major content area. We recruited consultants with national reputations and—more importantly— state-of-the-art perspectives on teaching and learning in the content areas to provide expert guidance and a fresh point of view that would help teachers think beyond the status quo. Though facilitated by consultants rather than by the teachers themselves, this work session was in many ways similar to those that had preceded it. Teachers were actively engaged and they addressed key curriculum questions—in the case of English language arts, "How does language learning develop between the time children begin school and the time they graduate?"

In their first attempt to design a curriculum framework addressing this question, language arts teachers took an activity-centered approach. They looked at the kind of experiences students should have at various levels in each of five areas—reading, writing, talk and drama, literature, and media—and identified key issues and common themes for consideration at each developmental level. The product was a matrix of prototypic activities to mark a broad path for language learning, K-12.

Meanwhile, planning began for the fourth and final session of the curriculum study. That session addressed these bottom-line questions:

- How great is the discrepancy between the curriculum we now have and the curriculum we want?

- How extensive is the work needed to develop guides that will help translate our new vision into reality in each subject, K-12?

- Where should we start?

- Upon what high-priority grade levels and subjects should the 50 curriculum writers first concentrate their work?

- What should be accomplished by the end of the first year, by the end of the second, and by the end of the third year?

Decisions on priorities for curriculum development may have been agonizing, but they were hardly surprising. It was agreed that the new curriculum needed to influence all levels—elementary, middle, and high schools—and that it needed to start where *students* start on each level. Planners decided that all four major content areas needed serious work, and that this work needed to be coordinated—indeed integrated. Thus, the master plan developed at this final study session and ratified by teachers across the district called for curriculum development to begin at the primary level with kindergarten and first grade, at the intermediate level with third grade, and at the high school level with ninth grade.

Developing the Guides

The fifty teachers chosen for full-time curriculum writing not only had experience at the targeted levels; they had a strong commitment to Project ACCESS and the confidence of their advisory committee colleagues who helped select them. Although newly separated from students they cared about and faced with a daunting set of deadlines, these teachers reported to their new assignments in mid-February eager to begin. The first few days were devoted to team-building, personalizing and organizing workspace borrowed from a corporate neighbor, and making decisions about how and when the work would flow.

As writing teams got down to specifics in developing objectives, strategies, units, and activities for particular subjects and grade levels, they continued to need the best help available. Though both willing and able to offer that help, curriculum directors took great care to be neither obtrusive nor intrusive in doing so. That first year especially, they did a great deal of what I like to call "leading from behind." On some days, that meant providing a sounding board and asking pointed questions. On others, it meant bringing in just the right book or article or sharing curriculum models gathered from other school systems. As work progressed, it often meant offering suggestions and acting as friendly critics.

In the case of English language arts, the most difficult design issue was—and continues to be—the scope and sequence that organizes instruction year-by-year and course-by-course. In Texas, where education is so highly regulated and accountability driven, a veritable laundry list of so-called "essential elements" must be incorporated into local curriculum in every subject on every grade level. Failure to do so explicitly was the reason our guides had failed the state accreditation review in the first place. We had known from the outset that it wouldn't be easy to reconcile the state mandate for explicit teaching of discrete objectives with the district's commitment to more integrated, experience-centered approaches to learning.

I still marvel at what this first group of teacher-writers accomplished in less than five months. It took two of these months to generate prototype materials that might be included in each section of each guide being developed that first year. Somehow, all this was written and compiled into a detailed interim report, then printed and distributed to schools for review and response. Again, representatives to the curriculum advisory committee were asked to meet with colleagues on their faculties or in their departments to collect feedback before the committee reconvened in mid-April.

Though overall response was positive, teachers in the field identified several areas of concern. Popular demand caused the K-12 goals identified for science to be changed completely. In language arts, reading had to be beefed up at the primary level as did literature at the high school level. Support for integration of reading and writing was equally strong. And there was strong support for interdisciplinary approaches.

Bolstered by the advice and consent of their colleagues, the writers returned to work. The writing of every section of every guide began with collaborative planning by grade-level and subject-area teams. Though the actual writing was parceled out to individual team members, consultations were frequent. After peer review, drafts went to technical writers and suggested revisions were returned for team approval before going to final layout.

Materials developed through this process included six six-week sections per guide—each including objectives, one or two sample units, and a collection of suggested activities. These sample units are the strongest encouragers of the kind of instruction to which Project ACCESS is committed.

In English, our units range from kindergarten materials helping students learn "All About Me" through talk and children's literature to middle school activities on "Exploring the Unknown" (the *unknown* referring to the world of the middle school) to a ninth grade "People Are People" multicultural, multidisciplinary study of art, music, architecture, and language.

Both literally and figuratively, the guides developed throughout this project have left plenty of space for individual teachers to make the curriculum their own. This point is made right up front in the orientation pages of every guide:

> This guide is yours. It is designed to be flexible and developmental. Add your favorite resources. Use it to create your own personal guide; it can develop with you.

To reinforce this point, we had the guides three-hole punched and issued in loose-leaf notebooks emblazoned with the Project ACCESS logo and the title *A Planning Guide for Curriculum.*

Making the Curriculum Happen

Curriculum, we are convinced, is much more than a set of guides: it is what actually happens in classrooms. Because our work in Houston is grounded in this premise, and because curriculum development continues to be so tightly linked to curriculum implementation, this account would not be complete without a description of the efforts to make Project ACCESS a reality in classrooms.

Though teachers must indeed continue to own the new curriculum, there is little doubt that administrators must buy into that curriculum if they are going to support it. For this reason, even before that first group of fifty teacher-writers went to press with their first set of guides, more than six hundred administrators participated in a two-day curriculum workshop. Several days in advance, each received a resource packet comprised of sections titled *Learners*, *Learning*, and *Leading*. Summer workshops, organized around these themes, involved administrators in examining their own assumptions, sampling current theory and research, becoming acquainted with the format and content of forthcoming curriculum guides, envisioning how the new curriculum might look in their own schools, and collaborating on strategies for initiating and supporting such change.

Since the first round of summer workshops, administrators have participated in periodic curriculum update sessions and undergone intensive training in collaborative leadership. Even so, much remains to be done and the search continues for ways to give principals, assistant principals, deans of instruction, and supervisors a greater stake in implementation of the new curriculums.

Because the ultimate experts on our curriculum are the teachers who developed it, they take the lead in introducing guides and helping their colleagues prepare for implementation. Because writers are encouraged to consider staff development needs as they generate curriculum materials, they have a stockpile of ideas with which to begin planning districtwide inservices. Sessions for language arts teachers, like those for teachers of other subjects, most often explore ways of transforming classroom culture to support the kind of learning encouraged by the new curriculum—learning that is active, collaborative, integrated, and reflective.

No one expected such a transformation to be quick, easy, or universally supported. From the beginning, it had been acknowledged that fundamental restructuring of curriculum is risky business: energies are taxed and results are slow in coming. Even as we anticipated the process of revising guides to reflect what had been learned in actual use, we were braced for perilous times. For starters, we had to face our superintendent's increasingly outspoken skepticism about the pervasive unit approach that integrated learning within and across content areas.

By the spring of 1990, that skepticism had been reinforced by another countercurrent with which Project ACCESS collided—escalating pressures for a quick-fix that would raise scores on an upgraded state test. As a result, teachers charged with responsibility for revising draft guides were directed by the superintendent to "disintegrate" content areas and delete all interdisciplinary units. Meanwhile, for all practical purposes, the curriculum in language arts and mathematics was being displaced by test-preparation booklets issued each six weeks with instructions for direct teaching of discrete state-assessed skills and pages of practice items. To make matters even worse, these top-down mandates coincided with a brutal power struggle over restructuring, especially over site-based management, which the school board favored and the superintendent resisted. As a result, Raymond's contract was bought out and, as the first year of curriculum revision drew to a close, she was slated to be replaced.

Did all this bring an untimely as well as unhappy end to the case study of curriculum development recounted on these pages? I think not. Although I recently retired from Houston schools to pursue other professional interests, I am told that plans for the 1991-92 school year call for developing supplements to revised guides that will again feature model units to integrate learning across content areas. Community organizations such as the Children's Museum are vigorously supporting these proposed plans with initiatives to expand programs involving hands-on, interdisciplinary learning. Of special note is Houston Grand Opera's new project to enhance children's learning in language arts through music, song, and drama. Meanwhile, as teachers and staff seek to bridge the transition to new leadership, reports abound that the new curriculum is alive, indeed robust, in an encouraging number of Houston classrooms. I am told that renewed energy is being devoted to developing and incorporating alternative modes of assessment, for example, portfolios to track progress in reading and writing, performance evaluation for oral presentations, and research projects.

The latter seems especially important. Not only can broader, more authentic means of assessment make the curriculum less vulnerable to expediencies of raising scores on high-stakes achievement, it can eventually allow the curriculum to be assessed on its own terms—the extent to which it does indeed make all learning accessible to all students, thus allowing the young people of our city to meet the ambitious goals set for our graduates.

References

ASCD. (1975). *The Middle School We Need.* A Report from the ASCD Working Group on the Emerging Adolescent Learner. Alexandria, Va.: Association for Supervision and Curriculum Development.

Barker, J.A. (1985). *Discovering the Future: The Business of Paradigms.* St. Paul, Minn.: ILI Press.

Gleick, J. (1987). *Chaos: Making A New Science.* New York: Penguin Books.

Haley-James, S. (1982). "Helping Students Learn Through Writing." *Language Arts* 59, 4: 726–731.

Kuhn, T. (1962). *The Structure of Scientific Revolution.* Chicago, Ill.: University of Chicago Press.

Lounsburg, J.H. and G.E. Vars. (1978). *A Curriculum for the Middle School Years.* New York: Harper & Row.

Merenbloom, E.Y. (1983). *The Team Program in the Middle School: A Handbook for Teachers.* Columbus, Ohio: National Middle School Association.

NMSA. (1982). *This We Believe.* Washington, D.C.: National Middle School Association.

PART THREE

A Curriculum Developer's Handbook

5 | An Assessment Base for English Programs

Language arts teachers have always struggled with program assessment and evaluation. It's not that they are unwilling to be assessed. Nor does their uneasiness with evaluation derive from some sort of antiscientific bias on the part of teachers who are generally more concerned with words than numbers. The difficulty with assessment in English has been three-fold.

First, a great many English language arts assessments have been standardized tests that rely on indirect indicators of language competence such as vocabulary, verbal analogies, and multiple-choice sentence correction exercises. As the field has moved more and more to a whole-language model, it has been increasingly evident that assessments of component sub-skills are not reliable measures of language competence. The NCTE has passed resolutions warning of the inappropriateness of various standardized measures of performance in English, but the effect of these examinations has been to hamper the growth and productive development of English language arts curriculums.

Second, standardized tests have been widely misinterpreted as measures of program success. In particular, the Scholastic Aptitude Test, a self-described measure of potential, not performance, has been inappropriately used by the press and general public as an assessment of entire language arts programs. Achievement tests and statewide assessments have been similarly misused. How many times have we read headlines on schools "failing to make the grade" based on measures that were never designed as curriculum assessment tools in the first place?

Third, the examinations often provide information too late to be of any use, serving as *ex post facto* sources of information that contribute little to instructional improvement.

We need to take the curricular bull by the horns and design assessments that can inform the curriculum process from the outset. In particular, assessment should precede and continue through curriculum development. It must be carried out using a variety of measures, including those developed by the teachers who create the program. In this chapter I discuss the types of assessments that can create a foundation for a new curriculum and in Chapter 8 I return to the assessment theme to show how such data can reasonably be "mined," not only to demonstrate program accountability, but to establish benchmarks of student achievement.

Creating a Curriculum Development Team

Who should do the assessing? Who, for that matter, should develop a new program? Standard—and effective—practice is to create a curriculum development team that includes but is not necessarily limited to:

- teachers from the grade levels/programs under review—volunteers, not a shanghaied crew that would rather be off doing something else
- the English language arts supervisor or coordinator
- community representatives—particularly those who are willing to inform themselves about language arts instruction
- a representative of the school administration
- a school counselor
- a board of education representative
- students

Naturally, the size and composition of the team will vary with the nature of the project. As we have seen from the Centers of Excellence, it's quite possible to create a one-person team for small projects, and it is equally possible to have a team that consists of all faculty members concerned.

The Present Curriculum

Assessment for curriculum development should begin with study of the program currently in place. The truly revolutionary curriculum developer may be tempted simply to disregard the old program and start from scratch, but traditional curriculum practices are inevitably used as reference points whether we intend for them to be or not. As the Centers of Excellence and curriculum narratives show, the savvy curriculum leader can often use present practices constructively when redesigning programs. Further, we must be careful *not* to cover the existing program with ashes prematurely—we need to know the *facts* about its content, successes, and limitations.

Here are some possible projects for the curriculum development team to undertake:

- Identify and describe the existing curriculum. Does it consist of a guidebook? the adopted textbooks? a montage of individual teachers' individual preferences? How does the present curriculum extend beyond its printed boundaries? What really goes on in individual classrooms and how do we know?

- List the elements of the present curriculum that seem most satisfactory, at least to a majority of the people who teach it. What are its strong points, its centers of excellence? (If the faculty were to take a visitor or an evaluation team on a tour, what sites or programs would be observed as best representing the existing program?)

- Poll teachers to identify specific problem areas. Find out where there is dissatisfaction.

- Identify specific projects or programs that would immediately lead to improvement in English language arts instruction. What would the faculty like to be doing or developing in English?

- Review the most recent external program evaluations (e.g., North Central, W.A.S.C., Middle States). Look for criticisms of the program and recommendations for reform. Discuss whether or not these are desirable, given the faculty's interests and commitments.

- Cautiously survey standardized test scores and other quantifiers that might shed light on the current performance of students in this curriculum.

- Create a list of target areas for change, expansion, and possible elimination in the existing program. Determine exactly how much change is needed.

- Daydream. Imagine the best-of-all-possible-worlds language arts curriculum. What would it achieve for the students? What and how would they learn? How would teachers assist that learning? What resources and facilities would be available to support the program? Then analyze the daydream for first principles—what does the daydream tell us about what we want for our students in the very real world?

Assessing Community Needs and Interests

An inadequate community-needs survey of the language arts can be disastrous. Too often, community members seem to want an updated form of the English they hated as children; they cling to old memories, even bad ones. Assessment of the community is critical, but it must be done in a way that educates community members while collecting data from them.

The curriculum developers might undertake some of the following projects to help educate and poll the community:

- Create a newsletter or fact sheet, publishing highly readable descriptions of new and interesting topics in the language arts. (The *ASCD Curriculum Update* series provides an excellent model for writers.) The newsletter might feature descriptions of such concepts as whole language, invented spelling, editing as a route to correctness, and the decline of the red pencil.

- Conduct informal workshops or information sessions on the new curriculum directions in conjunction with school gatherings such as parent-teacher meetings.
- Send community representatives to state, regional, and national meetings of English language arts teachers. Invite a parent to attend a summer writing institute. Include the community members of the curriculum team in faculty inservice programs.
- Interview parents about their concerns for their children. Include parents whose first language is not English and parents whose dialect is not fully middle-class, standard English.
- Interview representatives of the business community to help bridge the traditional gap between business and schooling.
- Engage the media. If appropriate, get a media person on the curriculum development team, not simply for public relations, but as a specialist in language and communication. At a minimum, send the media copies of newsletters, minutes, and meeting announcements.
- Arrange for secondary school English and history classes to write histories of the community. Possible topics include neighborhoods, ethnic groups, business growth and development, and the school system itself. These data can be shared with the community and used as background for curriculum development.
- Do a formal needs assessment of the community. What do parents see as important in teaching literacy? What do they value in their schools? What do they feel is wrong? In what ways do they feel satisfied with literacy instruction? In what ways do they believe it needs to be improved?

Several different survey instruments may be designed for sampling subpopulations in the district. The survey should target community members' views on: (a) the functional use of language in business and personal settings, (b) their aspirations for children in terms of careers and college and what they see as the language skills needed for each, and (c) their ideas for possible new developments in English language arts education in the district.

You may need the services of a good survey maker or research specialist to create an instrument that elicits the kind of information you want. Parents might be supplied with a list of goals to be ranked or given an open-ended questionnaire that allows write-in suggestions. Surveys can be distributed by mail, sent home with students, or published in the community paper. [For additional ideas on community/home involvement in curriculum see Dillon (1989) and Brandt (1989). Each offers a variety of perspectives on engaging parents as more than token advisors in school affairs.]

Student Needs and Abilities

The heart of the curriculum process is serious assessment of youngsters: what they can do with language, where their interests lie, and how their skills are developing. English curriculum specialists such as Patrick Creber (1965), James Moffett (1968, 1973), and David Jackson (1982) have called for programs that mesh patterns of student growth and development with the global aims of English language arts instruction. Creber (1965, p. 10) believes that curriculum cannot create "a dichotomy between the interests of the pupil and the interests of the subject." We need to explore the natural connections between youngsters' growth in language and the skills and knowledge we expect them to master in the language arts.

In recent years we've heard too many unsubstantiated claims about language decay: "Nobody uses sentences anymore." "Kids nowadays can't spell a single word or dot an i properly." Newspaper headlines and letters to the editor are no substitute for research. Fortunately, language arts educators have developed a number of informal measures that can be used to create a profile of student learners (Baskwill and Whitman 1988, Johnston 1983, Searle and Stevenson 1987, Taylor 1990).

The curriculum development team should collect some of the following pieces of data and develop measures of its own to gather additional information on students:

- Writing samples. Students' writing may be the single best tool for assessing what young people know and value. (Of course, not all students are *writers*, so one must interepret cautiously.) The curriculum committee should examine journals, informal writings done in class, polished papers, fiction, poetry, prose, and nonfiction. This writing should come from students of the widest possible range of abilities, including students whose native language is not English. From this writing, the committee can develop profiles of the students in the local school district. It is not appropriate simply to describe the error patterns in writing. We must look for answers to questions such as:

  a. What (written) language skills do our students generally exhibit successfully at each level of schooling?

  b. At what points, if any, do we see major leaps or changes in their writing? To what do we attribute those changes?

  c. Given a blank sheet of paper and an invitation to write, what sorts of themes, topics, and concerns do youngsters address? What patterns emerge?

  d. What crossover can we see in ideas expressed in exposition and in imaginative writing?

  e. How do children use writing as a tool for exploring their own world and the world around them?

- Transcripts of individual conferences and interviews with students.

Invite students to explore:
  a. their view of "language": What is it? What is it good for?
  b. their choice of subjects for schooling: What, most of all, would they like to study?
  c. their vision of how the English language arts program should be conducted.

Use these interviews to assess students' oral language skills as well. What evidence do we see of growing articulateness across the grades? Do our students have problems explaining themselves to adults? Where do they seem to fit on a spectrum of language skills from childhood talk to fully mature adult discourse?

- Information about reading interests. Monitor the titles being checked out of the library (with appropriate protection of individual rights to privacy). Keep lists of books in circulation from in-class language arts libraries. Find out what kids are reading on their own. Use these data to create a developmental profile of students' reading interests. Correlate the findings with the results of the writings and oral language interviews.

- Personal accounts. Have some students write a "literacy biography" (Taylor 1990), describing how they learned to read and write, their struggles and successes with literacy, and their views of its importance.

- Recheck the standardized test scores—last in this sequence—to see what additional helpful information such data can supply in creating a school language profile.

Staff Interests and Imperatives

English teachers vary widely in skills, interests, and educational backgrounds. Yet curriculums are often developed in a generic pattern suggesting that virtually any teacher can plug in to the program in any slot. Such an approach may work in a high paradigm subject like mathematics, but it is far less successful in a more subjective field like the English language arts. Instead of simply asking teachers to vote on curriculum or textbook choices, a curriculum development team should know the interests of the teachers as well as those of the community members and students.

The curriculum development team should:

- Conduct a formal survey of faculty views about program strengths, weaknesses, and needed changes. Data should be compiled and the findings published.

- Develop a faculty profile of expertise in teaching the English language arts. Each teacher has special skills: teaching poetry, coaching young writers, exciting youngsters about classical literature, and, yes, teaching grammar. All such skills should be identified.

- Initiate reading groups to discuss important new books in the teaching of English and important new books generally,classics of children's and adult literature, and new titles in children's and adolescent literature. Have these reading groups report regularly to the curriculum planning team.

- Create study teams to learn the state of the art in such areas as oral language, reading and literature, writing, language study, and media. Review the recent literature in such publications as *Language Arts* and *The English Journal.* Create a professional reading library.

- Send representatives of the faculty to summer institutes such as the National Writing Project, summer seminars of the National Endowment for the Humanities, or programs at nearby colleges and universities.

- Delegate faculty members to attend state and national conferences to learn about model programs elsewhere.

- Visit NCTE Centers of Excellence in English in your state.

- Meet with school administrators to discuss their perceptions of the current language arts program, its successes, failures, and needed new directions. Determine whether administrators are interested in and feel qualified to participate directly or indirectly in new curriculum and program development.

The curriculum development team should try to answer questions such as:

- What kinds of students do teachers work with most successfully? Granted, some teachers would simply like to cream off the perceived brightest and best, but other teachers have marked success working with other youngsters: kindergartners or fifth graders, non-native speakers of English, gifted and talented, remedial, and developmental students. Those special talents and interests should be acknowledged in the curriculum.

- What literatures do teachers enjoy and know most thoroughly? Who are the experts in fairy tales, myths and legends, short fiction, adolescent literature, modern poetry, films, or the literature of music?

- Do faculty members write? (If they do not write, they probably ought to enroll in a summer writing institute.) Have any faculty members been published in professional journals? Have some written for children or for the local newspaper? How can their skills be used in developing and teaching in a new program?

- What inservice and staff support do teachers actively want in order to teach the English language arts more successfully?

67

- What do teachers see as the school or curricular conditions that would let them teach more successfully? What are the current barriers? How can the curriculum be designed to accommodate or enhance people's natural teaching interests?

Creating an Agenda for Curriculum Change

To wrap up the assessment phase, the team may:

- Create a specific plan for curriculum reform, including, but not necessarily limited to:
  a. creating a general calendar or timetable
  b. developing plans for revision and adoption of aims and goals
  c. establishing needed subgroups, subcommittees, and working parties by interest or grade level
  d. getting outside help as needed
  e. arranging for curriculum leaders to attend vital meetings, workshops, and institutes
  f. making provision for released time or summer employment to create materials
  g. designing an evaluation plan

The curriculum agenda should also include plans and procedures to document the curriculum development process, including assessment. Create a "paper trail" that will not only reveal the rationale behind the program, but show the inner workings of the curriculum development group as well.

There is no fixed pattern for English language arts programs. Each curriculum must be developed to reflect local needs and interests (and state and national expectations). We must focus on "process" rather than "product." With a carefully compiled assessment base, the curriculum team is in a strong position to develop the specifics of such a plan or curriculum.

References

Baskwill, J., and P. Whitman. (1988). *Evaluation: Whole Language, Whole Child*. Richmond Hill, Ontario: Scholastic.

Brandt, R.S., ed. (October 1989). "Strengthening Partnerships with Parents and Community." Theme issue of *Educational Leadership* 47, 2: 4-67.

Creber, J.W.P. (1965). *Sense and Sensitivity in Teaching English*. London: University of London. Reprinted by the Exeter University Curriculum Center, St. Lukes, School of Education, Exeter, U.K.

Dillon, D., ed. (1989). "Home-School Relationships." Focus issue of *Language Arts* 66, 5: 14-51.

Jackson, D. (1982). *Continuity in Secondary English*. London and New York: Methuen.

Johnston, B. (1983). *Assessing English: Helping Students to Reflect on Their Work*. Sydney, Australia: St. Clair Press.

Moffett, J. (1968, 1973). *A Student Centered Language Arts Curriculum*. Boston, Mass.: Houghton Mifflin.

Searle, D., and M. Stevenson. (March 1987). "An Alternative Assessment Program in Language Arts." *Language Arts* 64, 3: 278-284.

Taylor, D. (February 1990). "Teaching Without Testing: Assessing the Complexity of Children's Literacy Learning." *English Education* 22, 1: 4-74.

6 | The Curriculum Framework

In *Émile*, Jean Jacques Rousseau offers what many would consider to be the ideal curriculum framework: a one-on-one arrangement with a tutor and child, so that the two explore ideas as they came up, moving from one topic to another into increasingly complex subjects. Today, for a variety of reasons, we choose to put students together in classrooms of twenty to thirty-five and in schoolhouses holding two hundred to four thousand students. With this congregation of kids and teachers comes the need for a curriculum that accommodates individual needs within larger structures and hierarchies.

Because of its link to experience, the learning of language is necessarily individualized, but only since the evolution of a growth-through-English philosophy have we begun to fully appreciate the dichotomy—even the paradox—that exists between curriculum and the individual reader-writer-listener-speaker. The difficulties have increased exponentially as our school population has become more diverse, including youngsters whose cultural background is not the same as their teachers' and whose native tongue may not be English. Teachers want to give their students a literacy program that responds to particular needs and patterns of development, but it is very difficult when dozens of children, *not* just like them, are all demanding attention.

The difficulty of trying to serve diverse students is even greater in oversized English language arts classes. It's one thing to struggle with meeting individual linguistic needs in a modestly sized classroom of, say twenty to twenty-five students, but it's much more difficult in larger classes. After careful deliberation, the NCTE has recommended that English language arts classes be limited to twenty-five students (with a maximum of four such classes for each secondary teacher). NCTE's periodic surveys show, however, that this class size is found in very few schools.

Larger classes not only make the teaching of writing more time consuming by adding to the traditional burden of theme correcting, they also complicate individualized learning in reading and oral language. And the current pedagogy in English clearly calls for highly individualized learning. The days of children spending most of their time reading a single book in common, writing on set theme topics, and reciting or discussing answers to teacher-centered questions are waning.

Ironically, the growth-through-English pedagogy does *not* support the Rousseauesque ideal of a strict one-to-one teacher: pupil ratio. Tutors may be needed for students with particular language problems or for those who need help mastering English as a second language, but for most children, language arts is clearly a *community* subject, requiring an exchange of ideas. The classroom becomes a place where children learn as much by interacting with one another as they do from the teacher.

The English language arts curriculum developer, therefore, confronts several crucial questions:

How can we treat language as *individualized* when we must teach clusters of youngsters all at once?

How do we realistically select materials, knowing that few books are appropriate for *all* children? How can we present common learning without forcing children to study inappropriate material, which is detrimental to their growth as readers?

And if we are successful in individualizing, how do we organize instruction in a rational way and measure its results?

The task of selecting a framework for English, then, is more than discovering a geometrically attractive structure for the curriculum, more than breaking standard content into grade level clumps, and more than divvying up adult language skills into measurable objectives.

Stating Your Program's Philosophy and Goals

In the heyday of the accountability movement, English language arts teachers were rightly taken to task for the vagueness of their aims: They wanted youngsters to "appreciate" literature, to become "lifetime readers," and to write "clearly"–all very difficult aims to measure. English educators, therefore, have encountered problems with precise measurement as they begin developing their research base. Problems in stating a philosophy and aims have been complicated by conservatism in the profession, so that even as we discuss a "new," individualized, organic, student-centered language arts program, some English teachers are firmly committed to practices that originated with teaching Latin in medieval monasteries.

Many curriculum study groups disregard the need to state a philosophy and aims for curriculum. They want to get on with the business of selecting texts or planning units of instruction. Who reads the statement of philosophy in a curriculum guide, anyway? Yet, if we ignore this stage we do so at the risk of creating a spineless, eclectic program or perhaps surrendering curriculum design to textbook writers. We also want to avoid the Scylla and Charibdis of creating either an apple pie statement of philosophy, agreeably phrased in generalities that everyone can accept, or a statement of aims that restricts, alienates, or ostracizes teachers.

A well-developed statement of philosophy and aims is more than a formality or curriculum developer's curious ritual. If done seriously, such a statement can provide genuine focus for teachers; it can even become something teachers use to enhance their understanding of a coherent program.

The assessment base recommended in the previous chapter helps solve some traditional problems of declaring philosophy and aims. If the curriculum development team has collected the kinds of data suggested, it has amassed important information for creating a curriculum framework. It need not generate aims at whim. It can base its discussion on the documented needs and interests of the school and community.

Here are some projects that curriculum development teams can undertake to establish a philosophy and aims:

- Define terms. What does the curriculum development group mean by statements of philosophy? aims? objectives? How do such statements relate to one another and to a curriculum? What sorts of statements does this group see as necessary to adequately outline its directions and intentions? Let me propose that *philosophy* represent a statement centering on the group's carefully researched convictions concerning how language is learned; that *aims* (or *goals*) focus on the overall scope and achievement of a school (or grade level); and that *objectives* describe specific accomplishments for individual units of study. In framing a curriculum, philosophy and aims come first: What are we trying to accomplish and why? (The development of specific objectives and benchmarks of achievement are discussed in Chapters 7 and 8.)

- Choose a format for statements. A useful model of aims statements is offered in "The Essentials of English," distributed by the NCTE, which lists a half dozen major goals for each activity area in English: reading, writing, listening, speaking, and so on.

- Debate the general statements of aims for English proposed by such groups as the English Coalition (reprinted in Appendix A), the NCTE, and the state or regional accrediting agency. Invite all faculty and interested parents to participate. As time permits, individual sections of such documents might be duplicated and distributed with requests for comments and reactions, for example, a passage dealing with oral language or with young adult literature.

- Obtain copies of curriculum guides and aims statements from schools that have produced exemplary curriculum guides in English. (See Appendix B, which lists the criteria for such guides. A current list of schools with exemplary guides is also available from NCTE, and many of the guides themselves are available on microfiche in ERIC.)

- Begin drafting a statement of philosophy and aims. The statement of philosophy should be tentative, containing the faculty's best description of what an English language arts program should contain. It should consciously incorporate supportable goals from the existing curriculum and make explicit how the new statement subsumes, adapts, and evolves from school or district traditions, particularly traditions of excellence.

- Take draft statements to the public early. Send newsletters to parents. Put a summary videotape on community cable television. Solicit comments and responses to the initial identification of philosophy and goals.

- Discuss all draft statements with faculty members who will teach in the program. Discuss your rationale as well. Let there be no suspicion of a hidden agenda.

Curriculum Patterns

The choices for a curriculum pattern are myriad. The "tripod" model is solidly established in many U.S. elementary and secondary schools. But alternative designs that are more consistent with contemporary theory are also being employed. These patterns, described below, are applicable at most grade levels.

Tutorial/Independent Study

This is the Rousseauesque ideal. I don't know of any school that has implemented a total independent study design for English language arts study. Nor would such a design necessarily be desirable, because it would eliminate communities of language learners, leaving the student talking only to a tutor. I describe the tutorial/independent study model here to anchor one end of the curriculum design spectrum. Under this plan, students would read and write on topics of their own choice with guidance from a teacher/tutor. While the design abolishes classes as we now know them, students might still meet in groups from time to time.

Although tutorial/independent study might not seem practical or desirable for a whole school or system, it bears careful consideration as a planned curriculum component, K-12. Can kindergartners do independent study? Of course they can; they learned to speak and listen under precisely that sort of tutorial model. Kindergartners, too, are quite capable of picking books to read or examine, selecting topics or themes for study, and executing reports on their learning through art, music, dance, imaginative play, oral language, and even elementary writing. The curriculum would not only encourage students to do independent work but also provide students the skills to step out into the world and to find resources for themselves. A possible outcome of a K-12 curriculum might be an independent, senior year, one-semester project in which students demonstrate the cumulative effect of language instruction. This sort of project is a better competency test than any standardized measure of minimum skills.

Reading/Writing Workshop: Whole Language

The process approach to writing and the newer definitions of reading have helped teachers—especially at the elementary level—develop strategies for approaching literacy in workshops that are quite close to the tutorial/independent study model. In writing workshop, students generally select their own topics, write at regular intervals during the week, and master a routine of prewriting, drafting, revising, and proofreading. Youngsters proceed at their own pace, consulting with their teacher and peers for advice.

In reading workshop, students pursue titles of their own choice, share their reactions with teachers and peers, and integrate reading and writing through responses to their reading. Teachers have developed management skills for such programs so they can accomplish the difficult task of monitoring individualized reading and writing programs of thirty or more students at once (Atwell 1987).

When reading and writing workshops are taking place concurrently, they naturally blend into a whole-language curriculum in which students may be diversely engaged in reading or writing (and talking, doing media work, and so forth). Although the whole-language model is in widest use at the elementary level, it is increasingly popular in senior high schools and even in college classes. There is no reason why one cannot construct an entire K-12 curriculum along the principles of whole language. The traditional objection to such a plan is that students won't choose the "great" books as they grow older or that their writing skills will stagnate and remain indefinitely at the level of narrative and personal experience. Developmental theory, however, argues that students do, in fact, mature and seek out increasingly more complex reading and writing. It would be interesting to put whole language to a K-12 test.

The Negotiated Curriculum

In the negotiated curriculum, students and teachers work together to set goals, choose materials, and design activities (Boomer 1982, Clarke 1989). Negotiation skills are not developed automatically, and students must be taught "to teach themselves" (Lindsey 1988). Although we could use negotiation as the essence of a full program (Gladman and Mowat 1986), a more feasible approach is to combine elements of negotiation across the curriculum or to place negotiated work toward the end of the school year after students and teachers have become skilled at working with one another. I am uncomfortable with the term "negotiated," which, in the United States, has connotations of adversarial confrontation and forced or resigned compromise. A better phrase, I think, might be a "student/teacher curriculum" or, perhaps, "*Emile* in the classroom."

Thematic/Topical

In this approach, student work is organized around content themes or topics such as "Dinosaurs," "Stars," "Geography," "Family," "Who Am I?"

"Minorities in Literature," "Science and the Future," and "Cities," to name just a few. Thematic/topic teaching is an especially useful and flexible way of organizing teaching and curriculum planning K-12. Teaching by themes gives a curriculum focus, allowing teachers to select some materials for common study. Themes or topics include almost infinite room to accommodate student interests and needs. Thus, a thematic program can easily incorporate elements of the negotiated curriculum, independent study, and reading/writing workshop, permitting individual students and groups to strike out in their own directions.

Generally, a thematic or topical unit, course, or curriculum will involve some reading of core selections (often works that are a bit too difficult for individualized study), a wider cluster of materials for small-group study, and a still wider range of individualized reading and study materials. Students read about, discuss, and write about central ideas as a whole class, but as they become familiar with the dimensions of the topic, they move increasingly into their own specialized work. As a child advances through the grades, themes are arranged in broad sequence from concrete to abstract, from concerns in the immediate world of the child to broader, global aspects of human interest.

The assessment base of Chapter 5 can easily be expanded to create the pattern of themes for even a K-12 curriculum. As the curriculum study group discovers the types of books students read and the sorts of topics they choose to write about, clusters of experiences and interests emerge, and teachers can begin to identify topics for study. Another, more direct way to approach it is to ask students what they would like to study. As students describe their concerns and interests, ranging from the ubiquitous dinosaurs in the elementary grades to human values in the upper grades, themes for investigation, reading, and writing quite naturally emerge.

Great Books

Great books or "masterpieces" courses focus on selected titles in literature, with discussion, writing, and drama emerging from these books. It is important in organizing such a curriculum that the great books be selected to mesh with students' developmental needs and interests; the books must not become an imposition. The Britannica-sponsored Great Books and Junior Great Books programs emphasize discussion pedagogy, with participants working out meanings for themselves rather than being driven to standard interpretations. A great books approach lacks the continuity of, say, a thematic approach, where ideas and texts are linked together. Further, there is potential danger through overemphasis on a book's alleged "greatness," which may restrict the range of possibilities or lead to the inclusion of classic-but-inaccessible materials. A better approach would be to develop a K-12 curriculum around a student-centered selection of "good" books. One could do even better by making great books, good books, and lots of other books available for class, group, and individualized reading.

Communication Skills

A contemporary version of "the tripod" is a communication skills curriculum that is structured around the processes of reading, writing, listening, and speaking (rather than at the static fields of literature, language, and composition). The processes of language are distributed developmentally by grade level so that students engage in activities and strengthen the skills that are appropriate to their age and ability. The curriculum developer's question then becomes, "What sorts of reading, writing, listening, and speaking activities are appropriate at each grade level?" The assessment base of Chapter 5 provides solid research for such a distribution of language processes.

Although such an approach is clearly student-centered and developmental, it can result in fragmentation of the language arts into discrete skills. One can easily wind up teaching a unit in speaking followed by isolated units in writing, reading, and listening. It can even lead to a very narrow basic-skills approach, with teachers itemizing the elements of the communications skills and teaching them one at a time.

A communication skills curriculum also runs the risk of being divorced from content: What is the substance to which students apply their reading, writing, speaking, and listening skills? If we answer that question and describe substance, we can easily make the error of assuming that content exists independently of the language used to express it.

Interdisciplinary

High on my list of curriculum preferences is the interdisciplinary language arts approach. The language across the curriculum movement has encouraged English teachers to think about language in other disciplines, and those teachers can also take a reciprocal view, introducing the content of other disciplines into their programs. In elementary school self-contained classrooms, interdisciplinary language arts work is quite natural, with students reading and writing on a wide range of topics in science, mathematics, social studies, and other fields. Middle schools also have a healthy interest in interdisciplinary and team-taught courses. High schools and colleges seem more reluctant to introduce interdisciplinary materials because of perceived problems of coverage: How can we cover all the literature students need to know?

The fact is, interdisciplinary curriculums offer intriguing possibilities for coverage. For example, one can look to the themes for study proposed in *Project 2061* (AAAS 1989). Although the program was designed expressly to teach science, I invite English language arts teachers to imagine the coverage of a K-12 *literacy* program centered on such themes as: "The Earth and Its Universe," "The Living Environment," "Human Organisms," "Human Society," "The Designed World," "Historical Perspectives," "Habits of Mind," and "Common Themes: Systems, Models, Constancy, Change, Evolution, and Scale." We might also envision an English language arts curriculum growing from the interdisciplinary themes proposed by the Bradley Commission on History in Schools (Jackson 1988). These include "Civilization," "Cultural Diffusion," "Innovation," "Human Interaction with the Environment," "Values, Beliefs, Political Ideas, and Institutions," "Conflict and Cooperation," "Major Developments," and "Patterns of Social and Political Interaction." English language arts teachers can consider the obvious interconnections between the topics proposed by the historians and scientists and the fundamental role of language and literature in exploring any of these themes at virtually any grade level in the schools.

Language Centered

Charles Suhor (1987) has proposed a curriculum based in "semiotics," the study of sign and symbol. In such a program, coherence would be gained by focusing on the rich variety of language that students can use to express ideas from their "experiential store." In some respects, this program would be linked to the communication skills approach. However, it would not only integrate the four basic language skills of reading, it would open up connections with media study and use and even symbolic arts such as painting and graphics. The program would also include careful consciousness raising so that students become increasingly aware of their control over language systems.

In reality, most new curriculum approaches, including whole language, reading/writing workshop, thematic/topical, and interdisciplinary are already language centered, having subsumed the traditional study of grammar under the much broader rubric of a language-in-use philosophy.

Humanities/Core

One of the better established interdisciplinary programs in the schools centers on English as a humanities study. English/social studies/history courses have been explored in various combinations for over half a century. The danger of such programs is the temptation to "go chronological," so that literature serves as a mere illustration of history, with composition reduced to literary/historical analysis. At its best, a humanities core focuses on questions of vital significance to all youngsters (and adults): Who am I? What does it mean to be human? What are my connections with humankind? All of literature, art, music, and drama centers on such questions, of course.

Global Studies

Philosophically linked with the humanities, global studies programs are naturally interdisciplinary. If we are to take the ideal of pluralistic, multicultural education seriously, a global education component must be a part of the curriculum. Complaints about the provinciality of American education can be remedied, in part, by infusing a wider range of international literatures in the language arts program. As global studies proponents forcefully argue, these programs are critical as the world continues to shrink and as American

77

youngsters are increasingly faced with the potential and promise of working and living in international settings. Given the centrality of language in human affairs, the language arts provide a natural base for the development of global studies projects.

English Within the Arts

Peter Abbs (1982) argues *against* English/humanities linkups, presenting the case that such ties reduce English to an historical footnote or to a gloss on human affairs. He sees language as an outgrowth of human imagination, and he wants to see English more closely aligned with the fine arts: music, dance, drama, art, and sculpture. Abbs includes both literature and composition in his program, stressing that the child is both a recipient of and a creator of the arts. Abbs's philosophy could lead to an arts-centered curriculum standing on its own, an idea not likely to sit well with job-minded taxpayers, but one that can be successfully factored into most of the curriculum designs presented here.

Chronological

Not on my list of recommended designs, the chronological approach—beginning with the oldest and most distant literature and proceeding to the present—is probably the most common one in American senior high schools, immortalized in generations of commercial anthologies focusing on American and British literatures. This model owes its domination to the influence of colleges and universities (where it is more appropriate for students who have made a decision to study literature for its own sake) and to pressure applied by the universities to prepare students for college English.

I have few positive things to say about this approach. Even as a way of covering traditional or canonical literature, it is weak in contrast to a humanities, thematic, global studies, interdisciplinary, or English within the arts approach. It exaggerates the role of history in literary achievement while diminishing the response and responsibility of a reader to the text.

The Tripod

Also failing to make my recommended list is the tripod, for reasons discussed in Chapters 1 and 2. To break English into literature, language, and composition units is simplistic. Nevertheless, even with the tripod it is possible to jury-rig elements of a personal growth or student-centered curriculum. For example, one can find interesting and engaging interdisciplinary topics within historical periods of literature (say, "Science and Morality in Victorian England"); or one can infuse a semiotic interest in language across all components of a tripod curriculum. Nevertheless, with the exciting potential that alternatives offer for curriculum development, there seems to be little to be gained with a model whose theoretical legs have already been knocked down.

Electives

As I discussed in Chapter 2, the elective movement in English language arts had a powerful effect on secondary school English programs before fading rapidly under pressure from the back-to-basics movement. In some respects, a program designed around electives can be a *non*curriculum that permits individual teachers to teach their specialties without a great deal of regard for making connections with others. Nevertheless, a curriculum group might strongly consider sequenced elective programs that focus on students as developing users of language. Interesting elective programs are also possible within, say, an interdisciplinary curriculum of the sort proposed by *Project 2061*. Or one could create a series of electives focusing on different world cultures and literatures guided by a global studies philosophy and framework.

Putting the Design Together

Any curriculum development group must conduct research into these and other schema. The group must forge a design that will be suited to the school or district, drawing, as before, on its assessment base. There is no national design that will suffice for all schools, no single program that will invariably work. My aim here has been to outline possibilities; the imaginative and disciplined task of integration of designs must be done by the curriculum developers and users.

However, if I were a member of your curriculum development team, I would lobby for arrangements such as the following for a K-12 program:

- K-3: A whole-language, reading-writing approach, highly individualized, with emphasis on initial engagement with literacy.
- 4-6: Interdisciplinary thematic units integrating language arts, science, social studies, mathematics, art, and music.
- Middle/junior high school: Focus on English within the arts, aimed at helping youngsters be powerful, imaginative users of language. I'd also introduce a language-centered emphasis here to help students become more conscious of language as a tool for personal, imaginative expression.
- Early senior high school, grades 9-10: Focus on communication skills through carefully designed thematic units centering on the students' emerging sense of self within a larger world.
- Later senior high: Electives, including courses with disciplinary and interdisciplinary foci in global studies, humanities, and science as well as courses with a literary theme: great books, themes in American literature, and topics in British literature.
- Last semester, senior year: Independent senior project in English.

That's one educator's dream. Your committee will need not only to dream, but to translate that dream into a curriculum.

References

AAAS. (1989). *Project 2061: Science for All Americans.* Washington, D.C.: American Association for the Advancement of Science.

Abbs, P. (1982). *English Within the Arts.* London: Hodder and Stoughton.

Atwell, N. (1987). *In the Middle.* Exeter, N.H.: Boynton/Cook.

Boomer, G., ed. (1982). *Negotiating the Curriculum.* Sydney, Australia, and New York: Ashton Scholastic.

Clarke, M. (April 1989). "Negotiating Agendas: Preliminary Considerations." *Language Arts* 66, 4: 370-80.

Gladman, S., and B. Mowat. (1986). "An Alternative to English." In *English Teachers at Work,* edited by Stephen Tchudi. Upper Montclair, N.J.: Boynton/Cook.

Jackson, K. (1988). "Building a History Curriculum." Report of the Bradley Commission on History in Schools. Washington, D.C.: Educational Excellence Network.

Lindsey, C. A., Jr. (1988). *Teaching Students to Teach Themselves.* New York: Nichols.

Suhor, C. (1987). "Toward a Semiotics Based Curriculum." *Journal of Curriculum Studies* 16: 3, 247-257.

7 | Development and Implementation of an English Language Arts Curriculum

Let's imagine the curriculum guide as beginning with an empty three-ring binder. After all, we've seen and toted around thick curriculum guides, implemented after intensive labor on the part of curriculum developers. Too often, such documents remain unused by faculty members, especially those who had no stake in their preparation.

The three-ring binder starts out *empty* and sends a message to all teachers in the system: You're to fill this with materials that will help you teach more successfully. That the curriculum guide is loose-leaf, not bound or stapled, implies that the curriculum is always in the process of development. Pages may be added and taken out, one at a time; the system isn't locked into a single document.

Now, I don't want to be taken too literally on this three-ring binder idea. Although I think a notebook is better than a bound guide, there are many formats a curriculum guide can take to be implemented successfully. My point is to emphasize that the guide (or whatever collection of documents a school uses to describe its program) ought to be *teacher developed, cumulative, constantly building,* and *subject to regular revision.* (Appendix B is a reprint of NCTE's "Criteria for Exemplary Curriculum Guides." It suggests what a screening committee of NCTE looks for when it assesses and evaluates guides. That document may prove useful as an illustration of what a curriculum binder might contain.)

Actually, we already have a start on filling the binder. Chapters 5 and 6 explored the development of documents that should be duplicated, three-hole punched, and distributed to teachers for discussion:

- a statement of aims and goals for the language arts within the school or district
- a summary of the group's assessment base for the new program, including capsule profiles of student interests and needs, community concerns, and teachers' perceived skills and areas of expertise
- an overall map of the curriculum design, whether whole language, interdisciplinary, thematic, or even the antique tripod
- a timetable and set of procedures for developing new programs

The binder might also include an engraved invitation to teachers to submit three-hole-punched documents for inclusion in the notebook.

Developing Instructional Units

An effective approach to creating materials is to invite development of pilot materials for eventual use in the curriculum binder. I once taught in a high school where teachers could design and teach pilot or experimental courses with a minimum of red tape, without having to write detailed course proposals for submission to a district curriculum screening committee. A teacher who had an idea—be it an approach to journalism or a thematic literature course—would write up a short description, receive approval from the committee, then teach the pilot course. The teacher could experiment with the course twice, then was required to come back to the curriculum committee with a full-scale proposal, including sample syllabi and pieces of student work, in order to have the course evaluated and approved as a standard curricular offering. This pilot approach treated teachers as responsible professionals, and in that school, a wide range of excellent, innovative courses have been developed.

Another school where I served as a consultant established a "unit builder's collaborative" for its teachers. Instead of creating a standardized K-12 curriculum, it blocked out a broad curriculum plan, then invited teachers to develop pieces, creating their own curriculum materials. The units that individual teachers pioneered in their classes were then duplicated and made available to other teachers in a variation of the three-ring-binder curriculum. In a short time, the district compiled a rich collection of teaching materials that allowed teachers to draw on their colleagues' previous efforts. The unwritten rule was that you couldn't draw on the stockpile until you had contributed to it yourself.

Both plans were highly successful at moving curriculum out of the stone tablet era toward that of the three-ring binder. Both projects were also based on the belief that if teachers are to be independent of textbooks, they need to create patterns of sharing resources among themselves.

Several projects can be initiated to fill the binder.

- Create and publicize a common unit format. Characteristically, a unit will include:
  — aims and objectives
  — materials and a list of related books
  — core and individualized activities
  — a general timetable
  — methods of assessment and evaluation
  A format should not be restrictive. It should allow for the writing needs of individual unit developers. The best way to settle on a format is for the members of the curriculum team to develop a unit, discuss its format, revise it, and publish it as a sample.

- Create teaching teams to develop portions of the new program and pilot variations of new units, courses, or a whole year's work. Ground rules for pilot projects need to be established, of course. Groups should be willing to show precisely how a project fits into the curriculum design and to describe how results will be assessed.

- Create a network among pilot curriculum groups. Many will be facing similar problems at similar points in the curriculum development process. Establish a newsletter in which curriculum groups describe their efforts. Even better, establish a computer bulletin board or electronic mail network so teachers can correspond quickly and easily. (In a pinch, use a plain old cork board in the curriculum library.)

- Circulate copies of professional articles that focus on appropriate aspects of curriculum development. Many journals automatically grant not-for-profit recopying of articles. Check the copyright statement and distribute copies of significant articles, three-hole punched, of course.

- Begin publishing teacher-developed units and materials. Label everything "Experimental Edition." Put these in the curriculum binder.

- Frequently update experimental editions as courses and programs evolve.

The board and administrators need to provide time for teachers to do curriculum work—during summer workshops, inservice days, or by reducing teaching loads. Without time for teachers to work on projects, the curriculum will follow conventional lines, probably those laid down by the textbook. The board and administrators should also set aside funds for purchasing classroom sets of new materials for use in experimental programs.

The pilot approach is a sensible middle ground between the grassroots and top-down approaches. Common observation suggests that the curriculum is, in the end, what teachers do in their classrooms, with or without an overall guiding curriculum document. At the same time, nobody wants to see the autonomy of the classroom carried to such an extreme that teachers operate in utter isolation, possibly following principles that conflict so greatly that

83

sustained growth becomes unlikely for students. A pilot approach, operating within a broader curriculum framework, assures that the curriculum has general coherence while recognizing that good individual teachers, in collaboration, can develop the materials that make a curriculum successful in specific settings.

Finding the Materials of Literacy

Too often, textbook selection is a major outcome of the curriculum process. The English language arts have a rather sorry history of curriculum that is dominated by commercially prepared textbooks. It may well be that a curriculum development group will find that textbook adoption is an essential or desirable part of curriculum revision. There are strong arguments that a high-quality text can serve as a focal point of the curriculum without dominating it, and there are good commercial products on the market, despite the general conservatism of the textbook industry.

If a group does decide to adopt a textbook or series, the assessment base of Chapter 5 and the curriculum goals and framework of Chapter 6 are essential to thoughtful selection. Does this text or series offer literature selections that are in line with what we know of our students' interests and abilities? Does it use real literature, preferably whole selections, rather than author-constructed materials and excerpts from longer works? Does it integrate writing and literature? Does it do more than pay lip service to such ideas as process writing, response to literature, and whole language? Does the text lend itself to *our* curriculum design, or will we find ourselves teaching to its formulas? (Lillian Hassler's curriculum narrative in Chapter 4 shows a curriculum group skillfully making precisely this sort of assessment.)

Sound textbook adoption processes for the English language arts have been developed (Tchudi and Mitchell 1989). As whole language and reading workshop approaches are increasingly used, however, we may well see a decrease in formal textbook adoptions. The Centers of Excellence reports include frequent mention of "real books," a curious expression that means teachers are turning to individual trade books rather than to "unreal" texts. Further, the curriculum of the future will focus on providing students with the richest possible range of materials of literacy, some of it in conventional print form, some of it coming to students through wires, satellite transmission, cathode ray tubes, and optical lenses.

Teachers engaged in a quest for new materials should:

- Become specialists in books for children and young adults, exploring and reviewing new and classic titles in fiction and nonfiction. They should engage the school librarians or media specialists in this quest and urge them to obtain titles that complement the English language arts curriculum.

- Involve parents in reading and recommending titles for use at all grade levels. Such a practice has two major benefits: It provides relief for teachers already too busy teaching to do extensive additional reading, and it gives community members a solid stake in the literary materials used in the schools.

- Form a liaison with the education director of area newspapers and integrate a Newspapers in Education program into the school. Curriculum planners should ensure that plenty of copies of each day's paper are available to any teacher who wants to use the up-to-date resource of the morning's current events and topics.

- Meet with paperback book distributors to explore ways of getting a range of books and magazines into the school at low cost in the manner described by Fader and McNeil (1968).

- Create a book review group of students. As you begin to pick and choose literacy materials for the program, consult frequently with the consumers and invite their assessment of your choices.

- Form a subgroup to explore how television can be used as an integral part of the curriculum. For example, the group might suggest ways in which programs ranging from sitcoms to documentaries can fit into the themes identified by the curriculum planning group.

- Create a research team to look into videos, particularly those with ties to reading, and to investigate ways of upgrading the school or district media collection.

- Encourage faculty members in fields other than English to suggest major titles in their areas—books for children, young adults, and adults. Develop interdisciplinary holdings in mathematics, science, the arts, history, social studies, and vocational or applied fields.

- Conduct research on electronic and optical storage and retrieval systems, including computerized library programs, so that your school can link up with other sources.

- Study electronic networks and bulletin boards that put students in touch with other people and information sources worldwide.

- Conduct a community "scavenger hunt" for the materials of literacy. The curriculum developers should look to community service agencies, businesses and industry, local and state governments, business associations, and service clubs for print and visual materials and for support in getting more materials for the school program.

The Teacher-as-Researcher

In the past decade, the concept of "teacher-as-researcher" has empowered English language arts teachers, giving them control over their own teaching. An important book on this topic carries the significant, descriptive title *Reclaiming the Classroom* (Goswami and Stillman 1986). The teacher-as-researcher gains new power over teaching, a sense of ownership of instruction that is not always possible if curriculum is set by outsiders, whether a curriculum development group or a textbook author.

The teacher-as-researcher movement emerged as a by-product of the interest in writing-as-process. As teachers came to see writing as a way of confirming, exploring, and creating knowledge for their students, they discovered they could use it the same way to explore their own teaching.

The teacher-as-researcher is, above all, a *writer*. Such a teacher designs questions about curriculum and teaching, creates trials or experimental lessons and activities, collects a variety of evidence, and *writes up* findings. The data collected by this teacher/writer/researcher are wide-ranging:

- questionnaires, surveys, and attitude scales administered both pre- and post-instruction.
- journals and learning logs
- papers, projects, and imaginative writings
- anecdotal records and classroom stories
- formal student evaluation of individual activities, literacy materials, and whole units
- test scores of teacher-made or standardized tests

While gathering these data, the teacher keeps a learning log, recording and analyzing in the manner of the ethnographic researcher, as a participant observer.

Teacher research in English language arts is not scientific in the traditional sense. There are no experimental and control groups, no detailed compilations of statistics. Critics argue that because there are no controls, teacher research can be highly subjective, with researchers seeing and finding only what they were searching for in the first place. While acknowledging the subjectivity, supporters claim that through careful data collection from several sources, from the process of writing itself, and, above all, from a teacher's willingness to share results with a larger community, one can arrive at "truths" that are highly significant in teaching and help individual teachers and colleagues in ways that are quite impossible within the constraints of formal educational research.

I have seen powerful results emerge from teacher research projects: experiments with alternative grading systems in English, trials with more and less written feedback on written composition, studies of the content of student journals and the implications for formal writing, and investigation of alternative approaches to correctness in student writing. Teacher researchers do not make claims that their findings can be applied to larger and larger populations (that task is left to other teacher researchers working in their own contexts). Rather, the researchers simply try to show, in depth, what they did, thought about, and observed. For most readers/colleagues, the "proof" or validity of such research is not found in numbers or evidence, but within the written narrative itself: Does this story ring true?

Teacher research, then, can be an integral part of developing new curriculum units and materials. Teachers and curriculum leaders can:

- Learn about the teacher researcher approach. Locate English language arts teachers in the region who have explored the idea and learn about their techniques and approaches.

- Build teacher research into pilot programs, making evaluation a constant part of the process of curriculum development. The result will be an unusually well-documented curriculum, one that clearly answers such questions as: "Why are we doing this?" and "Does it work?"

- Publish abstracts or summaries of teacher research documents in the curriculum newsletter, as always, three-hole punched for the binder.

- Conduct inservice "fairs," analogous to "science fairs," in which teachers display the products of their research: the notebooks, the student writing, and the evaluation forms from students.

- Create a study group to look for links between local classroom research and national research issues. Such journals as *Research in the Teaching of English* and *Language Arts* regularly publish research articles and summaries on topics of interest to classroom teachers. By checking their own results against those described in the national journals, teachers can validate their efforts.

Securing Community and Student Support

Support for a new language arts program needs to be secured at many points in the process, not simply at the conclusion when a new curriculum is unveiled to the public.

One of the greatest failures in English language arts curriculum change in recent years came about because of a failure to adequately inform communities. The focus of change was the bugbear of *grammar*. Reading the professional research, teachers came to realize that they had been overemphasizing grammar in their classes, that it wasn't producing results. However, teachers often failed to explain that as they diminished grammar lessons, they were increasing the amount of writing youngsters were doing in the classroom, including innovative techniques such as peer group revision, individual proofreading, and mini-lessons on particular usage problems. Teachers were still working hard on correctness and standard English, yet because they failed to inform the public clearly, there is a widespread perception that English teachers no longer care about standard English, that they permit and even encourage "sloppy" writing.

The kind of curriculum described in this monograph requires careful explication for the community. It won't be centered in the formalist tripod that many community members recall from their own school days, and it may have some of the trappings of the much feared and little understood "progressivism." A contempory, forward-looking English curriculum will focus on such ideas as interdisciplinarity, whole language, and thematic teaching, with emphasis on oral language, media, and language-across-the-curriculum. It can easily fail to receive support if it surprises the taxpayers.

The approach using the pilot program and the teacher-as-researcher provides a wealth of possibilities for securing community support. More than that, it can actually engage students and community members in the curriculum process by:

- Engaging parents as researchers. The quest for parental input into the curriculum should not end with the initial community surveys to establish the assessment base (see Chapter 5). Every pilot/research group can collect information from parents—reactions to plans, proposed books and readings, and writing projects. In the process, curriculum writers will simultaneously be informing parents about the scope of the program.

- Engaging students as researchers. Give students increasing responsibility for assessing their own learning and the means by which that learning is taking place. The teacher-as-researcher model emphasizes collecting large amounts of data from the students' journals, logs, papers, and examinations. By relying on student input, the researcher helps ensure that students will be well-informed about what is happening in their curricular lives.

- Publishing examples of student work created under new programs. Publication can be as simple as a classroom newsletter, student written and edited, explaining and documenting what's going on. Or it can be a district publication on new directions in English language arts programs.

- Engaging parents as tutors, aides, and advisors in the program. Most parents are far more literate than they think and can productively serve as readers and responders to student writing, as reading coaches, and as storytellers. They can do this in school as volunteer tutors, but they should also be encouraged to lend a hand at home. An issue of a teacher-to-parent newsletter can focus on ideas and techniques for helping parents serve their children better. For example, parents should be told not to rewrite their children's papers; they should be taught to raise questions that will help their children see for themselves the parts that are unclear. Even parents whose native language is not English, or whose dialect is different from established standards, can serve helpfully as respondents to their children's work (and in the process, develop their own language skills).

Implementation and Professional Development

The curriculum process described here does not have a single moment of implementation, a time when (presumably with appropriate ceremony) a new program is said to be "in place." As teachers and groups of teachers complete new materials, subprograms, and thematic units, each of those will come on line.

A key to successful growth and sustenance of the program itself rests with opportunities for continued professional growth. Teachers need to talk about what's happening in their classrooms; they need to remain in touch with national trends and issues; and they need external support from consultants from time to time (the clichéd "shot in the arm").

Some suggested implementation and staff development activities include:

- creating an English language arts bulletin board in the faculty lounge for student writing and other work, recent newspaper articles, and fliers for upcoming conferences and workshops.

- establishing a local reading group on children's or adolescent literature, possibly including parents and students, to review new titles and to slot these into appropriate places in the new program.

- bringing in speakers to address the concerns of *this* faculty. Most English language arts teachers have had their fill of outside speakers with set topics and inspirational routines. What's needed for curriculum nurturing are outsiders who will listen to problems described by faculty and assist in finding solutions. Consultants may also prove helpful in observing the program and simply validating that what's going on is appropriate and productive.

- setting up exchange visits with other districts or schools (or even within individual buildings). It's astonishing how seldom experienced teachers observe others teaching. An exchange program, even if only done a few days a year, tends to infuse a curriculum with new ideas while validating its directions.

- encouraging teacher-researcher/curriculum developers to publish their ideas and achievements whether in the local newspaper, the state language arts newsletter, or a national publication such as *Language Arts* or *The English Journal*.

- hosting regional or state workshops on your new program, sharing, not only the final product, but the route to that achievement.

- identifying the greatest centers of innovation and excellence in the new program and applying for recognition from the NCTE. One can apply for the Centers of Excellence Program and submit curriculum materials to the Committee to Review Curriculum Bulletins.

As the three-ring binder fills, the curriculum design takes shape and gains substance. Housekeeping is required from time to time to keep the binder fresh and up-to-date. Obsolete materials must be tossed; new materials must take their places. The binders themselves may even wear out, due, one hopes, to their constant use as a guiding force in the program.

References

Fader, D., and E. McNeil. (1968). *Hooked on Books: Program and Proof.* New York: Berkeley Medallion.

Goswami, D., and P. Stillman. (1986). *Reclaiming the Classroom.* Exeter, N.H.: Boynton/Cook.

Tchudi, S., and D. Mitchell. (1989). *Explorations in the Teaching of English.* New York: Harper & Row.

8 | (Re)Assessment of the Skills and Standards of the English Language Arts Program

Traditionally, one stakes out standards of achievement at the goal-setting stage and then designs a curriculum to ensure that the standards are met. But the language arts are unique among the disciplines of the school curriculum. Because of the nature of language and its interconnections with human growth and development, the English program should reflect student achievement with language in an environment conducive to language growth, rather than being driven by standards of achievement derived *a priori*.

Further, English programs call for a high degree of individualization. In a writing workshop, students often select their own topics (or choose from a wide variety offered by the teacher); in reading class, they select their own books, often from an array offered by the teacher or the media specialist. With such an approach, it becomes extraordinarily difficult—even naive—to prescribe standards in advance of achievement.

Nevertheless, we *can* observe what happens when students approach literacy in an organic English curriculum, especially if that observation is done through the teacher-as-researcher model. Patterns emerge. Some books work well with kids year after year; others don't. Students appear to be readier for some language tasks than for others at various times in their lives. Youngsters master the skills of language following observable patterns.

The curriculum process I describe here does not ignore skills or diminish their importance. Rather, it places them at an appropriate place in the program, as *outcomes* of a curriculum rather than as the elements that structure it. In fact, this skill-outcomes program is quite likely to reveal development of abilities far beyond the limited lists usually offered as starting points or minimums. It is an approach that allows us to document the full range of youngster's language growth, rather than limiting instruction to a tiny range of it.

Assessing Skills and Linguistic Achievements

The use of terms like "skills" and "standards" to describe an English language arts program may be misleading and even obsolete. English educators once thought that language skills grew from knowledge of rules for proper grammar, rhetoric, and mechanics. We now know that language skills are extraordinarily more complex. For a child (or adult) to utter a simple sentence: "Mary bit the dog!" involves literally hundreds of identifiable language acts (or skills) including perceiving (seeing what Mary did and fitting it into mental/linguistic categories), critical thinking (realizing that something unusual has happened), framing a message for an audience (deciding to tell someone about this unusual occurrence), and putting it into actual language (which itself calls for understanding vast resources of words and sophisticated, if intuitive, rules for ordering them into comprehensible sentences). It's important, then, not to oversimplify the skills of language and not to act as if they are blocks stacked up to create total language competence.

It is equally important not to make the same sort of error about standards. Although people do conform to a variety of language rules, the number of such rules known by even the least skilled speaker/reader/writer is astronomical. Sometimes the word "standards" is used to apply to a few simple conventions of usage (or grammar), choices such as "ain't" versus "isn't," or "he don't" versus "he doesn't." But to call such choices "standards" or to imagine that they are anything more than the tip of the linguistic iceberg is to skew a program inappropriately and even doom it to failure.

I prefer to discuss "linguistic achievement" rather than "standards." This is not a mere euphemism or sophistry. It's a shorthand way of saying, "Let's describe what kids actually do with language as a result of our curriculum." Their achievement can be described at many levels and in a great many forms: by counting errors on students' papers pre- and post-instruction, by describing the range of their writing, by comparing papers completed across time, by listing books they have read, and by assessing results on standardized tests. Readers will recognize that in previous chapters we created a strong base for such measurement throughout the curriculum process, including establishment of the initial assessment base and the emphasis on teacher-as-researcher.

To document students' linguistic achievement in the new program, the curriculum committee can:

- Annually assess writing portfolios. Students should keep much of the writing they produce for a year, culling from it four or five pieces that represent the spectrum of their early and latter writing and demonstrate the range of discourse forms and modes that have been mastered. Teachers can then list the global skills or abilities that seem to be emerging.

- Do occasional whole-school writing assessments. Diederich (1974) has created a model for pre- and post-test analytic scoring, which has become an industry standard for the language arts. Simmons (1990) has shown how assessment can be extended to writing portfolios, thus not limiting the writing collected to timed sittings where every child writes on the same topic.

- Create individual reading records for children. These can be cards or file folders in which students list the books they have read. Look for growth patterns in students' reading as a way of documenting linguistic achievement.

- Conference with students (and parents), examining writing and reading portfolios and discussing what the student has learned and is learning.

- Tape record or videotape students' small-group and whole-class discussions from time to time. Use such data to describe oral language skills that are being developed.

- Create questionnaires and surveys that give students an opportunity to assess their own accomplishments with language. (Be cautious here. Like many adults, children often underestimate their language skills because of past emphasis on "correctness." Nevertheless, youngsters do, in fact, have a pretty good sense of what they can and cannot accomplish with language.)

- Create a school evaluation and assessment policy that clarifies the relationship between student achievement in language and the evaluation and grading procedures in the school. (The Canadian Council of Teachers of English has created an especially valuable statement on this topic, including the use of a variety of assessment tools. See Appendix C.)

- Invite graduates to return to school to discuss how their training in English has served them in business or college. (But interpret their remarks cautiously. Many returning students exaggerate their own deficiencies and suggest rather wistfully that the schools should have "done more" to help them with the linguistic demands of business or college.)

- Invite college admissions officers or English faculty members to discuss the expectations of area colleges and universities for entering freshmen. (Again exercise interpretive caution; the college folks tend to want everything taken care of in the schools, a not altogether realistic expectation.)

After all or most of the above have been completed, describe language skills that the students in the school or district seem to be developing. Create a descriptive skills list rather than a prescriptive or standardized list. Lists can be done by grade level, by school, or as a summative K–12 list. Perhaps the most important criterion for such a list is that it be genuinely informative to teachers and parents, showing them just what's being accomplished in English classes.

How many skills do you want to identify? At what level of specificity? Skills could be listed at the broad levels of reading, writing, listening, and speaking, or at varying levels within each of those categories. It might be useful to survey some of the exemplary curriculum guides published by NCTE to see sample lists. Half a dozen skills for each of the major language areas—writing, speaking, reading, and media—will suffice to show the public, students, and teachers what needs to be accomplished at each grade level.

Do not allow the skills list to become reductionist or to turn yellow in the three-ring binder. It should be reviewed yearly. And remember, it is a ‚ demonstrated end product, not a prescription for instruction.

Establishing Benchmarks

The term "benchmark" commonly means a standard against which performance is measured. However, the term originated in the field of cartography, where it described a permanent marker used by mapmakers to create reference points. That older definition is a useful metaphor for use in assessing the outcomes of a language arts program.

Each child in the school has an individual language topography: students' linguistic maps have heights and depths, curves and contours; they reflect experiences, interests, and education. Marie may be a skilled oral storyteller and writer of drama but less adept at expository writing. Derek may be good enough at reading newspapers and magazines but will not finish a piece of fiction, even one written explicitly for children at his grade level. Topography is descriptive rather than evaluative: It shows the lay of the land rather than lamenting the valleys and exalting the peaks. The teacher learns about students' topography by observing performance and keeping records of student journals and logs, writing portfolios, reading lists, individual conferences, and so on.

In assessment that moves beyond the individual student, we must continue to observe individual topographies while recognizing that classes and schools have topographies, too. A topographical map of a community shows every hill and gully; in a state or regional map such rises and dips become part of more broadly described features such as mountain ranges and plateaus. (Nevertheless, when you step out your front door, it's the gully that matters, not the overall height of the land.)

Through record-keeping and teacher research, we may be able to recognize topographical patterns of many sorts and at many levels, for example:

- The youngest children in the school work most successfully in oral and dramatic modes.
- Our fifth grade boys write most of their fiction patterned after current television programs and films.

- Our seniors seem to do well enough with argumentative prose, but have a difficult time integrating resources into their research writing.

David Jackson (1982, p. 239) describes "markers" (akin to "benchmarks") of student accomplishment in his developmental program for British secondary school students. He suggests, by way of illustration, that for eleven-year-olds teachers can expect to see:

- Pleasure in reading. Some gain reading confidence by exploring small books by themselves, for example, Betsy Byar's *The Eighteenth Emergency*, Paula Fox's *A Likely Place*, and F. P. Heide's *The Shrinking of Treehorn*.

- Clear and coherent thought about what they read when their curiosity is caught. Active interrogation methods (e.g., hunting for clues, arguing with books, etc.) can be helpful.

- The ability to work out their own personal contexts for what they read, often through other media like collage, drama, painting, murals, and so on.

Markers can be explicit and detailed, with as many illustrations, examples, and samples of student work as necessary. Jackson lists about thirty markers in language for each year in his curriculum scheme. That seems like a reasonable number to offer a very clear profile of linguistic development and performance.

Benchmarks provide a much more detailed topography than the conventional skills list, more specificity than the usual "global objectives" for a language arts program. Above all, they describe what children do with language rather than what we might wish they could do often without research evidence. Perhaps equally important, benchmarks are extremely useful to teachers at the next level of schooling because they also offer a glimpse of what children *might do next*.

John Dixon (1987) talks of "staging points" for language work. Everything that a child does with language is a staging point for a next step, a new achievement. A student who publishes a letter in the school paper may be ready to send a letter to the *Times*. The student who has completed an Arthur Conan Doyle story may be ready to tackle an Edgar Allen Poe work (or simply to move on to a more sophisticated Doyle story). So it is with larger scale topography: A benchmark that shows students doing well with narrative in grade nine might suggest that we move from that starting point to exploring exposition. Thus, assessment can focus as much on the potential for new growth as on present demonstrations of achievement.

External Standards and Examinations

Descriptive skills lists and benchmarks also help to solve conventional problems with outside norms. Language arts programs, no matter how good they seem on local assessment, operate within a context of national trends, developments, and measures of achievements. Any community or curriculum development group will spend some time discussing state assessments and nationally administered tests such as the National Assessment of Educational Progress, the Scholastic Aptitude Test, and the American College Test.

The weaknesses of such tests when used as measures of school system performance have been widely documented; they are not particularly strong measures of either student ability or school curriculum achievement. Yet, these tests not only persist but are allowed to establish benchmarks of a very different sort than those just described. Whether or not we particularly value them, standardized tests are, as the cliché rightly observes, "here to stay." They offer a reasonably convenient, reasonably inexpensive way to compare students and school systems. Therefore, they will continue to be held up as measures of performance.

It is important to understand that the benchmarks established by any well-designed English language arts program will easily encompass and exceed state, regional, and national standards. Putting it boldly, national norms and expectations do not pose a threat to the kind of English program described in this book. The new methods—writing-as-process, whole language, language across the curriculum, reading for meaning—all lead to observable improvement in language and to the establishment of clear and accurate markers of student performance. In contrast, the items tested nationally just skim the surface of the language pond, limited as they are in means of measurement and data processing.

It is natural, then, for a curriculum group to compare its benchmarks to national norms in order to see how the new program holds up. There may be some discrepancies, and a curriculum group may want to make modifications to ensure that students are receiving experiences that will ready them for the tests. This may even include occasional test awareness and test-taking lessons, perhaps the single best way to improve performance on examinations anyway. However, to reemphasize the point: A solid English language arts program that provides frequent, integrated, developmental experiences with a wide range of language skills is self-evidently the best way to ensure that students not only meet, but far exceed, external norms and expectations.

References

Deiderich, P. (1974). *Measuring Growth in English*. Urbana, Ill.: National Council of Teachers of English.

Dixon, J. (June 28, 1987). "English Education in London Programme." Lecture to the Michigan State University. Nutford House, University of London.

Jackson, D. (1982). *Continuity in Secondary English*. New York: Methuen.

Simmons, J. (1990). "Portfolios as Large-Scale Assessment." *Language Arts* 67 (March 1990): 23-27.

Postscript: The English Language Arts Curriculum of the Future

During the summer of 1989 I taught a workshop for Northeastern University as part of its Martha's Vineyard Summer Institute. The seminar explored "Literacy for the '90s," and its participants were fourteen elementary, secondary, and college teachers from around the country: Alaska, Texas, Oklahoma, Virginia, Ohio, and a number of eastern seaboard states. Although this group was not necessarily representative of all U.S. English teachers, its view of the major trends, issues, and problems that language arts curriculum leaders will face in the future is instructive.

We began the seminar by discussing the report of the 1984 conference of the International Federation for the Teaching of English: *Language, Schooling, and Society* (Tchudi 1985). This conference had looked at the state of the art in English teaching and identified priorities for future curriculum concern. Responding to the recommendations of international specialists, but within the context of their own teaching experience, the participants in my seminar identified five priority areas:

1. Student Diversity

At the international seminar, Robert Pattison (1985) of Long Island University had raised a difficult question: If Huckleberry Finn, a model of unschooled, non-book wisdom, showed up in our classes, would we try to "beat that out of him"? Would we, like Aunt Polly, try our best to civilize him according to our view of civilization (pp. 50-51)? Pattison's question centered on two issues: (1) whether teachers are willing to teach *all* students, even those who come from very different backgrounds, and (2) whether teachers are able to recognize that there are diverse views of "civilization" that don't necessarily mesh with their own. The Huck Finns among us may be less than enthusiastic about the purported values of traditional schoolhouse literacy.

My students said they would emphatically *not* try to beat Huck's natural wisdom out of him, and they were clear on recognizing its values. However, the question of what to do with, to, and for Huck in the classroom remains a puzzling one. My students were deeply concerned about the growing diversity of students in their schools and how to reach them. They described students who come from greater than ever racial, ethnic, and family diversity. They are concerned about students whose prior experiences with literacy range from near zero (the television and video game generation) to those with conventional middle-class reading/writing backgrounds.

The Martha's Vineyard teachers were also trying to accept the increasing numbers of new-age Huck Finns in their classes. A major priority for these teachers was to find new ways to invite their Huck Finns into fuller participation in a broad, humanistic, yet practical, literacy that accommodates a variety of learning styles and language dialects. There was strong opposition to any form of ability grouping and reservations about pull-out programs that allegedly help problem students by removing them from regular classes for isolated instruction. The implication was that without abandoning its own traditions, the English language arts program must considerably expand its dimensions and offerings in the coming decade.

2. Multiculturalism and Gender

In the United States, we've been acutely aware of the need to expand the contents of the curriculum for almost three decades. But progress is slow, slower than the changing nature of school populations, particularly in urban areas. My students hope to see multiethnic, multicultural literature representing both sexes included in the daily curriculum. It is not enough, they felt, to include the occasional token minority author or to isolate diverse literatures in the occasional multiethnic or multicultural unit. Further, they argued that teaching can be greatly enriched if teachers take full advantage of the exciting and diverse literatures that have been published worldwide. They were very critical of the advocates of "cultural literacy" such as E. D. Hirsch (1987), who seem set on centering the curriculum on what one student called, "the dead white guys."

3. The Electronic Age

Anthony Adams (1985) of Cambridge University, England, described a "New Athenian Age" in which electronic technologies open up a wealth of possibilities for work and leisure, with exciting potential for communication and artistic expression and engagement. Teachers in the United States are not hostile to the new technologies, but they are concerned about teaching students who live in a television/video culture. As one teacher in the Martha's Vineyard seminar observed, video stores are now far more common than bookstores in the United States; the impact on print literacy is undeniable if not easily measured.

My students favored increasing integration of all technologies (including old-fashioned book "technology") in the English classroom. In a satirical presentation, they role-played members of a New Athenian generation in which all students were comfortably media literate but had to be re-educated in fundamentals of reading and writing.

Several participants warned particularly of the danger of "old wine in new bottles," or, as McLuhan would have phrased it, "using the new media to preserve an old curriculum." Video and computers, for instance, will not make much of a change in language arts if they are employed to teach old-fashioned literary history or obsolete grammar terminology, no matter how visually attractive the presentation may be.

4. Politics and Power

English teachers have not been a particularly effective political force in the United States, at least in terms of classroom content and curricular teaching conditions. Professional organizations such as the NCTE have not been highly successful in working within political/legislative structures for productive curriculum change. Indeed, the English teaching organizations have often responded reactively rather than proactively.

My Vineyard students emphatically felt that language arts teachers must take a more active role in determining their own classroom destinies. To use the buzzword, they want "empowerment." They worried about colleagues who are not professionally active, who don't seem to have the time or the energy to labor in the political arena for more control over their own curriculum. While no clear or easy solution emerged, several participants stressed the role of the "reflective" and "responsible" teacher as a political as well as pedagogical force. They see the route to political influence coming about through an increasing commitment to a thoughtful, theoretically sound mode of teaching. My students saw considerable promise in the growing number of U.S. teachers who have participated in workshops like the Vineyard institutes, feeling that a growing body of well-informed teachers can make a significant difference in the future shape of the curriculum. They were also optimistic about the effects of the teacher-as-researcher movement, which has provided increasing numbers of teachers with the confidence and support to successfully make decisions about their own teaching.

5. The Integrated Curriculum

There was consensus at Martha's Vineyard that the English curriculum as a whole has not kept pace with exciting developments in separate areas of the language arts, particularly the process approach to writing and the response approach to reading and literature. In other words, although our profession has improved in teaching reading and writing, we have yet to create curriculums that fully and successfully merge the language arts into a whole language program. And my students did *not* try to design such a program—a curriculum for the future. Indeed, they argued against the current public pressure in the United States toward core curriculums, national standards, and state and national assessments. They felt that the best curriculums for the future will be based on a locally-desired concept, featuring a dazzling array of multiethnic, multicultural, multimedia literature and equally diverse opportunities to compose in print, oral language, and electronic technologies. However, they were pessimistic that substantial change in the curriculum is possible in the current conservative political/economic climate. They predict continuing change within individual classrooms, but frustration at school- or systemwide levels.

* * *

This group of teachers did a remarkable job of identifying issues for the future. However, progress on a grand scale will be slow, often impeded by short-sighted public, political, and media views of "proper" education. Schooling the public may be the highest priority of all if the English curriculum of 2001 is to look much different from that of today.

What remains is for leaders of the profession—in individual schools and districts and at the national level—to provide opportunities for thoughtful curriculum development. New curriculums cannot be created in crash programs. They cannot be mandated by external authorities. They cannot be implemented overnight. They will emerge over time, and their success will depend in no small measure on teacher empowerment coupled with necessary professional support including time and resources for program development. The potential for a "new English" curriculum by 2001 is considerable, but the barriers to reflective curriculum development are enormous. Strong and aggressive leadership is needed.

References

Adams, A. (1985). "Language, Schooling, and Society." In *Language, Schooling, and Society*, edited by S. Tchudi. Upper Montclair, N.J.: Boynton/Cook.

Hirsch, E.D. (1987). *Cultural Literacy*. New York: Harper & Row.

Pattison, R. (1985). "Literacy: Confessions of a Heretic." In *Language, Schooling, and Society*, edited by S. Tchudi. Upper Montclair, N.J.: Boynton/Cook.

Appendix A
The English Coalition Report
(National Council of Teachers of English/ Modern Language Association)

Assumptions

1. The language arts (reading, writing, speaking, and listening) are inextricably related to thinking.

2. Reading, writing, speaking, and listening are social and interactive.

3. Learning is a process of actively constructing meaning from experience, including encounters with many kinds of print and nonprint texts.

4. Others—parents, teachers, and peers—help learners construct meanings by serving as supportive models, providing frames and materials for inquiry, helping create and modify hypotheses, and confirming the worth of the venture.

5. All students possess a rich fund of prior knowledge, based on unique linguistic, cultural, socioeconomic, and experiential backgrounds.

6. Acknowledging and appreciating diversity is necessary to a democratic society.

Aims

1. To empower students:
   — as lifelong learners whose command of language is exemplary and who gain pleasure and fulfillment from reading, writing, speaking, and listening.
   — as active inquirers, experimenters, and problem solvers who are able to use the arts of language as a means of gaining insight into and reflecting upon their own and others' lives.
   — as productive citizens who use language to take charge of their own lives and to communicate effectively with others.
   — as theorizers about their own language and learning, able to read, write, and reflect on texts from multiple perspectives.

Reprinted with permission of the NCTE. The full Coalition Conference Report contains explanations of the rationale for these statements as well as descriptions of recommended teaching practices and institutional support. Summary leaflets are available from the National Council of Teachers of English, 1111 Kenyon Road, Urbana, Illinois 61801. (Stock No. 13591, Secondary; Stock No. 13559, Elementary). For more detailed discussions, see J.N. Jensen, ed., *Stories to Grow On: Demonstrations of Language Learning in K-8 Classrooms* (Portsmouth, N.H.: Heinemann, 1988) and R. Lloyd-Jones and A. Lunsford, eds., *The English Coalition Conference: Democracy Through Language* (Urbana, Ill.: National Council of Teachers of English and Modern Language Association 1989).]

2. To empower teachers:
— as active learners who serve as coaches, mentors, and collaborative creators of learning experiences rather than as dispensers of information.
— as decision makers in every aspect of schooling.
3. To integrate the arts of reading, writing, speaking, and listening throughout the curriculum.

Recommendations

The child and learning are at the center of any discussion of what English studies should be or how English should be taught. At the most general level, schools aim to help children develop into competent, knowledgeable, and self-confident language users. Such children *learn about* language; they *learn how* to listen, speak, read, and write; and they *learn why* language and literacy are central to their lives.

The Elementary Curriculum

1. Base the curriculum on sound research in child growth and development, psychology of language and literacy, language and literacy acquisition, as well as work in learning theory and the teaching of language and literacy.

2. Emphasize both content and process in the curriculum. The English curriculum is concerned both with what students need to know and with what they are able to do. Process is taught in a holistic way, stressing skills as a part of an overall process, not in isolation or as ends in themselves. In a similar fashion, the content of the language arts curriculum does not focus on particular facts, lists of literary works or characters, rote definitions of literary terms, or isolated language or literacy facts. Rather, content gives meaning to English instruction by providing an idea-oriented curriculum.

3. Link listening, speaking, reading, and writing in the curriculum and make them the focus of every subject area.

4. Recognize that commercially published materials provide only suggestions and should not become the curriculum.

5. Design assessments so that teaching and testing are brought together in ways that help teachers teach.

6. Develop curriculum within school communities of teachers and students.

The Secondary Curriculum

1. Assure that the English curriculum is flexible enough to adapt to outside influences and events and to relate to the ways language is used throughout the curriculum.

2. Emphasize both content and process in the curriculum. . . . [Language identical to #2 above.]

3. Study a variety of complete works of literature, as well as a wide variety of other texts, such as student writing, television, advertising, video, specialty magazines, film, and technical reports.

4. Invite students to read deeply in our diverse literary tradition, including writings by men and women of many racial, ethnic, and cultural groups.

5. Teach higher level thinking in conjunction with the regular English curriculum, not in isolation.

Appendix B
Criteria for Planning and Evaluating English Language Arts Curriculum Guides

NCTE's Committee to Evaluate Curriculum Guides and Competency Requirements has repeatedly revised its criteria in an effort to keep pace with the practices of the best curriculum developers. These criteria were formulated with several objectives in mind. First, they provide each member of the committee with a uniform basis for initial evaluation, with each guide also viewed as a unique document. Second, the criteria may serve to help schools and other educational agencies that are in the process of developing and evaluating curriculums. Finally, the committee hopes that the criteria may act as a change agent within the field of the English language arts.

Philosophy

This guide...

1. presents a statement of district or faculty philosophy that coherently conveys the beliefs of the developers about student and subject matter;

2. promotes a natural, organic integration of language arts experiences;

3. encourages teachers to view language as both a subject and a communicative process central to all human life and learning;

4. recognizes that individual processes of language development and concept development cannot necessarily be grouped into arbitrary grade level expectancies of requirements;

5. reflects knowledge of current or recent developments in modern language theory;

6. indicates that successful language experiences are essential for all students;

7. recognizes the assets of bidialectal, bilingual, and non-English-speaking students in exploring language concepts;

8. recognizes the importance of students' accepting their native language as well as that of others.

Objectives

This guide...

1. includes objectives directly related to the philosophy;

2. states objectives as tasks that can be performed;

3. recognizes that many objectives are desirable even though progress toward them may not be easily observed or accurately measured;

4. sets clear objectives for all major components of the English curriculum within the scope and sequence of the guide;

5. distinguishes teacher objectives from student objectives;

6. includes objectives that are varied and that accommodate a range of student abilities and teaching styles;

7. contains objectives for improving both expressive (writing and speaking) and receptive (reading and listening) language.

Content: Language

This guide...

1. recognizes that the content of language study often comes from real life;

2. provides for the study of a variety of conventional aspects of linguistics, such as semantics, regional and social dialects, grammars, lexicography, body language, and history of language;

3. provides for both imaginative and informative uses of language in student groups;

4. encourages student application of language appropriate to audience and purpose;

5. distinguishes between grammar and usage;

6. recognizes that acquiring information *about* language does not necessarily improve oral or written language performance.

Content: Composition

This guide...

1. suggests strategies for developing composition skills;

2. recognizes the significance of composing as a means of self-discovery and of bringing order to human experience;

3. recognizes that composing is a process involving stages, such as prewriting, drafting, and revising;

4. provides prewriting activities designed to stimulate composing;

5. recognizes that composing is often aided by small-group interaction in an atmosphere of sharing;

6. allows for student-teacher interaction (conferences);

7. recommends that composing occur for different purposes and usually for audiences other than the teacher;

8. recognizes that analysis of language is an editing tool in the composing process (improves editing).

Content: Reading

This guide...

1. provides ways to determine individual degrees of readiness;

2. suggests procedures to help teachers develop student reading skills;

3. recognizes that a total reading program, reaching beyond the development of basic reading (decoding) skills, focuses on student comprehension;

4. relates reading instruction to the whole language arts program.

Content: Literature

This guide...

1. provides for a comprehensive literature program;

2. provides for study of various literary genres;

3. recommends that students be allowed and encouraged to select and read all types of literature, classical through contemporary;

4. recognizes that involvement in a piece of literature is more important than talking about literary terms;

5. helps teachers to identify, explore, and accept varieties of affective and cognitive responses;

6. provides for the integration of writing and literature.

Content: Media

This guide...

1. promotes audiovisual as well as verbal literacy;

2. suggests ways of involving students in using media;

3. suggests specific media supplements for learning activities;

4. lists media resources available to teachers and specific procedures for obtaining them;

5. recognizes the use of the new technology (computers, word processors) in the teaching of English.

Organization

This guide...

1. suggests a scope and sequence of basic communication skills;

2. makes clear how particular units and lessons are related to the total English language arts program;

3. organizes major aspects of the language arts according to some consistent, identified structure or pattern;

4. provides a process for learning through which teachers help students become increasingly independent.

Policies and Procedures

This plan...

1. explains teachers' responsibilities and suggests options for content and methodology;

2. reflects the principle that students themselves should often generate learning activities;

3. reflects the participation of the total educational community;

4.regards textbooks as resources rather than courses of study;

5. supports the view that curriculum building is an ongoing process.

Design

This guide...

1. is easy to read: the language is clear and effective;

2. is presented in an appealing form and style;

3. has a format, such as loose leaf, that makes revision convenient;

4. states its relationship, if any, to other curriculum guides, district goals, or graduation requirements;

5. suggests as resources a large variety of specific background materials and school services;

6. provides a model for evaluation of the program.

Appendix C
Evaluation Policy
(The Canadian Council of Teachers of English)

Proficiency in English or language arts is reflected through many aspects of performance and attitude in both expression and reception: through speaking and writing on one hand, and listening, reading, and viewing on the other. It is characterized by habits such as reading and by critical judgment as applied, for example, to literature and to the veracity of information from many sources. Increased enjoyment as well as increased proficiency is an objective of the English program.

Principles

General

1. Evaluation, to be appropriate, must reflect in a balanced manner, the many dimensions of proficiency; assessment must not be limited to the testing of supposed "discrete" skills.

2. As far as possible, assessment should employ direct rather than indirect measures of achievement, and it may often concern process as well as product.

3. Evaluation should include the reporting of the prevalence of attitudes, habits, and interests.

4. Evaluation should properly reflect the curriculum. It must be balanced so that all major aspects of the program receive due weight.

Classroom

5. Students have the right to know the objectives of the program, the means of assessment, and the standards to be met.

6. Parents likewise have the right to know the objectives of the program and, in general, the expectations for the student. They must be properly informed of tests and other measures employed.

7. The teacher's judgment must be the main determinant of the performance of his/her students, and he/she will employ a variety of measures and observations to inform that judgment. Tests or examinations extrinsic to the classroom should play only a subordinate role in any determination of student achievement.

Statement prepared by Peter J.A. Evans, Director-at-Large, Evaluation, Canadian Council of Teachers of English. Reprinted in abridged form by permission.

External

(i) Commercial Standardized Tests

The following policy statements in no manner imply endorsement by the Canadian Council of Teachers of English of the use of such products: the statements have been created as advice to teachers and administrators where such tests are in use or their use is under consideration.

8. Any standardized test in use or being considered for use should be rigorously examined by a committee, which includes teachers responsible for that portion of the curriculum, with particular attention to **validity, norms and fairness, and the use to be made of scores.**

9. For all standardized tests or other external tests employed, each teacher, principal, or counselor making use of test data must be acquainted with the basis on which norms were developed and the error of measurement provided in the technical manual for the test, and ensure that scores are reported, used, and explained (to parents and students) in a manner that makes clear the limits of precision.

(ii) Design of External Evaluations: System or Province

10. Teachers and consultants, individually and/or through bodies such as curriculum committees, evaluation committees, and, more broadly, through their professional organizations, should have a substantial role in the selection, development, design, and administration of instruments, tests, or examinations intended for evaluation at the system or provincial level. Their role in the general design of the evaluation framework, especially in the form, scope, and distribution of reports, is also essential.

Appendix D
Survey Respondents
NCTE Centers of Excellence

Alamo Heights Junior High School, San Antonio, Texas (Kristine Reiman)
Albemarle County Public Schools, Charlottesville, Virginia (Mallory Loehr)
Bartle School, Highland Park, New Jersey (Harriet Schweitzer)
Beaverton High School, Beaverton, Oregon (Jack Huhtala and Teresa Brandon)
Bettendorf Middle School, Bettendorf, Iowa (Leo Schubert)
Center Senior High School, Kansas City, Missouri (Mary Lu Foreman)
Centerville Community Schools, Centerville, Iowa (Joan Hoffman)
Contoocook Valley School District, Peterborough, New Hampshire
    (Paula Flemming)
Ethel McKnight School, East Windsor, New Jersey (Carole Messersmith)
Evanston Township High School, Evanston, Illinois (Malcolm Stern)
Frenchtown High School, Frenchtown, Montana (Rick Unruh)
Glenbard West High School, Glen Ellyn, Illinois (Ellen Jo Lyung)
Hazelwood West High School, Hazelwood, Missouri (Anne Wright)
Henking School, Glenview, Illinois (Barbara L. Gabroshe)
Holland Hall School, Tulsa, Oklahoma (Stephen Kennedy)
Homewood-Flossmoor High School, Flossmoor, Illinois (Cheryl Kazlow)
John Jacobs School, Phoenix, Arizona (Merle Valenzuela)
John Jay Junior High School, Katonah, New York (Mary Winsky)
Kayenta Unified School District, Kayenta, Arizona (Tess Ritchhart,
    Gilbert Sombrero)
LaPerle School, Edmonton, Alberta, Canada (M. Dale)
Luther Burbank High School, Burbank, California (Jeanne Savoy, Bill Melton)
Madison Metropolitan School District, Madison, Wisconsin (Evelyn Berge)
Manwah Public Schools, Manwah, New Jersey (Mary E. Murphy)
Monroe Catholic Central High School, Fairbanks, Alaska (Kathleen Norris)
Monroe County School Corporation, Bloomington, Indiana
    (Helen Hollingsworth)
Moreland Elementary School, Shaker Heights, Ohio (Regie Routman)
Mt. Ararat School, Topsham, Maine (William J. Anderson)
North High School, Columbus, Indiana (Shirley Lister)
Pleasant Valley High School, Pleasant Valley, Iowa (Rex Grove)
Northern Arizona University, Flagstaff, Arizona (Peggy Ver Velde)
Paul D. Schreiber High School, Port Washington, New York (John Broza)
Providence Day School, Charlotte, North Carolina (Kathy Taylor)
Rock Bridge Senior High School, Columbia, Missouri (Michael Bancroft)
Rosell Catholic High School, Rochelle, New Jersey (Julius Gottilla)
Rufus King High School, Milwaukee, Wisconsin (Sandra Stark)
Sabal Palm Elementary School, North Miami Beach, Florida (Elizabeth Block
    Rubin)

Seaholm High School, Birmingham, Michigan (Jay Horshak)
Springbrook High School, Silver Spring, Maryland (Nancy Traubitz)
St. Michael's Catholic School, Marquette, Michigan (Sister Mary Ann Laurin)
Tenakill School District, Closter, New Jersey (Elizabeth Ziegler, Lynn Stampa,
    Jim Klika)
University High School, Urbana, Illinois (Audrey Wells)
Upper Arlington Informal Alternative Program, Barrington Elementary
    School, Upper Arlington, Ohio (Mark Carter)
Vicksburg High School, Vicksburg, Mississippi (Patricia Puia)
Wayne Central School District, Ontario Center, New York (Robert Berkowitz)
Weber Junior High School, Port Washington, New York (George Williams)
West High School, Wausau, Wisconsin (Greg Venne)
Westminster High School, Westminster, Maryland (Barry Gelsinger)
Ysleta Independent School District, El Paso, Texas (Ginna L. Rhodes,
    Sharon Knipp)

About the Authors

Stephen Tchudi is Professor of English at the University of Nevada, Reno, where he teaches courses in rhetoric and composition. He is a past president of the National Council of Teachers of English.

Lillian Hassler is an Elementary School Teacher in Fairbanks, Alaska. She has taught elementary and secondary school in Philadelphia and in Window Rock, Arizona (the Navajo Nation).

Carol Kuykendall is Adjunct Professor of Reading/Language Arts at the University of Houston, Clear Lake. She is former Associate Superintendent for Curriculum of the Houston Independent School District where she also served as Director of English Language Arts. She serves on the Curriculum Commission of the National Council of Teachers of English.

Jan Loveless is the Senior Instructional Designer for the Learning Center of the Dow Chemical Company, Pittsburg, California. She has taught secondary school language arts and science, and served as head of the departments of English and foreign language at H. H. Dow High School in Midland, Michigan.

Betty Swiggett is an Education Consultant. She is a former English Language Arts Coordinator for the Hampton, Virginia, City Schools. She has been a secondary teacher and a member of the faculties of Point Loma College, Old Dominion University, and The College of William and Mary.